LESSON PLANNING

Related Titles

Quantum Teaching: Orchestrating Student Success
Bobbi DePorter, Mark Reardon, and Sarah Singer-Nourie
ISBN: 0-205-28664-X

The Pocket Mentor: A Handbook for Teachers
Chris A. Niebrand, Elizabeth L. Horn, and Robina F. Holmes
ISBN: 0-205-29693-9

LESSON PLANNING

LONG-RANGE AND SHORT-RANGE MODELS FOR GRADES K–6

LINDA KARGES-BONE
Charleston Southern University

Allyn and Bacon
Boston • London • Toronto • Sydney • Tokyo • Singapore

Series editor: Francis Helland
Series editorial assistant: Bridget Keane
Manufacturing buyer: Suzanne Lareau

Copyright © 2000 by Allyn & Bacon
A Pearson Education Company
Needham Heights, MA 02494

Internet: www.abacon.com

Library of Congress Cataloging-in-Publication Data
Karges-Bone, Linda.
    Lesson Planning: Long-Range amd Short-Range Models
  for Grades K–6 / Linda Karges-Bone.
        p.   cm.
    Includes bibliographical references (p.   ) and index.
    ISBN 0-205-28627-5
    1. Lesson Planning.   2. Education, Elementary—Curricula.
  I. Title.
  LB1027.4.K37   1999
  371.3'028—dc21   99-18626
                                                            CIP

Printed in the United States of America
10 9 8 7 6 5 4 3   03 02

This book is for Gary, who knows more about planning than anybody else.
Happy twentieth anniversary in the new millennium.
This verse is for you: "And ye shall seek me, and find me, when ye search for
me with all your heart." Jeremiah 29:19 KJV

CONTENTS

PREFACE

This is a book for future teachers, novice teachers, experienced teachers (who may struggle with long-range planning issues that were not covered in their pre-service training), teacher educators, administrators, and curriculum designers. The purposes of this book are threefold: (1) to discuss the trends and issues surrounding planning for instruction and assessment; (2) to show teachers how to design plans that are organized, meaningful, and thorough; and (3) to demonstrate the techniques for planning by sharing sample plans that meet rigorous criteria.

Planning can be a joyful, creative process that brings teams of teachers together and that helps schools to chart year-long journeys for curriculum and instruction.

Good planning results in enhanced student achievement, polished teacher performance, and satisfied parents.

These end products do not come without effort and, dare I say it, a "plan." *Lesson Planning: Long-Range and Short-Range Models for Grades K–6* can give you and your school a template for planning that will make teaching and learning more enjoyable and productive.

WHO NEEDS THIS BOOK AND WHY IS IT HELPFUL?

As you explore this book on planning, you will follow a path that leads from long-range planning to short-range planning to daily planning. Each stop on the planning journey gives the teacher an opportunity to rest and regroup as well as to ask questions.

One question you might have as you anticipate this trek is, "Why might I need to know more about planning?" That answer depends on the amount of experience that you bring to this journey. Experienced hikers on a mountain trail will be able to cover more territory in a day, and with fewer provisions in their backpacks. The same analogy holds true for teachers. If you are an experienced teacher, you may already have a long-range plan "in your head." However, new evaluation and accountability procedures in your school may call for more formal, long-range plans. Or, you might simply want to review the procedures and examples in this text and, drawing on your wealth of experience, move in a new direction.

A novice hiker might require a guide, a heavily loaded backpack of sustaining trail mix, and extra socks to make the trip. A new teacher might need to use all of the forms and reproducible parts of the sample plans in order to stay on task and to meet school expectations.

In my opinion, the most helpful sections of this text are the samples of long-range plans (LRP), short-range plans (SRP), and daily plans. These plans were created by senior teaching interns who took my class on planning and have field-tested their products in real-life classrooms. The feedback from these teachers and their cooperating teachers has been positive. The novice needs the kind of structure and detail that these pages provide; they will also help those who are learning to plan either for longer periods of time or for diverse student groups.

The planning course to which I refer above is entitled Curriculum and Assessment, and it evolved from my dissertation research (1994) on authentic assessment. From this, I learned that both experienced and novice teachers struggle with assessment because, typically, assessment is not well covered in teacher education programs.

However, my analysis of the interview transcripts from that research also supported the need for more intense instruction in the art and science of planning, which leads to good assessment. The new course that I eventually developed became a hands-on, practical study of how to plan for both the long range and the short range, with an emphasis on the outcome or assessment of student learning.

This book, *Lesson Planning: Long-Range and Short-Range Models for Grades K–6,* evolved as students, from both the undergraduate and graduate schools, urged me to "write a book for us," taking what I had been showing and telling them in class and making it available to all teachers.

"All right," I agreed. "I'll write the book, but I want some of you to share your best plans as samples in the book so that other teachers can see that these procedures can turn into viable plans." My students rose to the challenge; the work of Sherri Malone Berry, Victoria Castagnaro, and Keyna Cooper Ferguson, all honor graduates of Charleston Southern University (CSU) and graduates of our teacher education program, is included in the sample sections. These novice teachers, and many others, field-tested their LRPs, SRPs, and daily plans in directed teaching and found that good planning was a critical element in good teaching.

It goes without saying that more experienced teachers might find the structure, length, and detail of many of the sample plans to be "overkill." But for novice teachers, for those moving into a new grade level or content area, or for those whose teacher preparation programs did not emphasize planning and assessment, these samples can be most helpful.

Finally, the appendix contains a glossary of planning terms because teachers asked for it. In my 1994 research, in the pilot years of ADEPT (the South Carolina teacher evaluation model), and in the first few semesters of my course, teachers in the field and in the training program made repeated requests for a "common language" in planning.

Planning is one tangible mark of a teacher's excellence. A teacher's skill in and commitment to planning will translate into polished instruction. The students' success and the teacher's feelings of confidence may be linked to planning. Planning is both art and science. It is a road map and a journey, with the destination left up to you and your students. As the popular car commercial invites…enjoy the ride!

ACKNOWLEDGMENTS

Special thanks to Frances Helland, my editor at Allyn and Bacon, who had a vision for this book and helped me plan for it over a two-year period. I would also acknowledge the work of Sherri Malone Berry, Victoria Castagnaro, Kenya Ferguson, and all the curriculum and assessment students at Charleston Southern University who have a passion for teaching. My gratitude is extended to Mary Antley, my administrative assistant, who has a unique talent for finding files that are hiding on data disks. My appreciation also goes to the following reviewers for their comments on the manuscript: Rebecca Downing, Olathe USD #233, and Carolyn Cadney, Biloxi High School. Finally, I would like to recognize the efforts of the South Carolina State Department of Education and especially Dan Linton, former Coordinator of the ADEPT program for its emphasis on long-range planning in the ADEPT model of teacher evaluation. My work in the pilot study of that program sparked my desire to create a book that would help teachers to become better planners.

CHAPTER 1

The Art and Science of Planning

How could one teacher handle sixty-seven squirming children?
How different the reality was from the way it had sounded in
front of Miss Alice's fire during our first staff conference with her.
At that time, she had asked Mr. Grantland to take over the Bible,
arithmetic and mathematics classes; I was to handle the rest.
Then Miss Alice had helped me plan a daily schedule. On paper
the plan had looked so logical. Now I was not so sure.

(From *Christy,* the story of a young teacher in Appalachia, by Catherine Marshall)

Like "Christy," the eager young schoolteacher depicted in Catherine Marshall's novel, I remember my first planning book. In careful, schoolgirl script, I wrote those first plans: "Math, Pages 33–34. Examples 1–20, even." That was about what it looked like, neatly entered in the sturdy, new, red leather lesson plan book. What grade level? Which textbook? Was I introducing fractions? Reviewing addition with regrouping? Doing a graphing activity? Practicing multiplication tables? Preparing for a test? Who could know? And what about those children? Did this "plan" reflect any kind of thinking about *who they were* or *what they brought to the experience?* As I look back, it was not really a lesson plan at all but was simply a page marker for the math book. And, like Christy, when I faced those squirming, expectant youngsters, I realized that teaching and the requisite planning that must come first would be much more complex and demanding than I had anticipated.

Since the early 1980s, I have taught special education, gifted education, "regular" (whatever that means) kindergarten, and college English; I also have spent a decade preparing new teachers at the university level. In between, I devoted a few years at home to teaching my two little girls to read, write, and negotiate the world of learning. I believe that all of these experiences moved me toward greater competency and creativity as a teacher. Earning advanced degrees helped a little bit, but not nearly as much as teaching two sections of kindergarten each day, with thirty-two children in the morning session and thirty-two more little ones in the afternoon session. An experimental stint in a noncategorized special education resource room, in which I taught children who had different disabilities (learning disabilities, emotional problems, moderate mental retardation, mild hearing or visual impairments) at one time, also gave me a chance to hone my skills. I learned two things quickly: (1) *Planning is everything* and (2) *be flexible in your planning.*

WHY PLANNING IS SO CRITICAL

A military officer friend of mine once explained his success as a leader in this way: "Plan your work and then work your plan." Although this graduate of a

1

prestigious military academy was relating his theory to the arena of war, I find curious connections to the arena of teaching and learning. Consider these facts:

> The cerebral cortex, unfolded, is about the size of a dinner napkin. But, if you were to begin counting the connections in the cortical sheet, at the rate of one synapse per second, you would finish counting some thirty-two million years after you began. (Dr. Gerald Edelman, in *Bright Air, Brilliant Fire, On the Matter of the Mind*)

The sheer complexity and enormity of the human brain makes careful, generous, creative planning a critical first step in teaching. Our growing wealth of information about cognitive science ("thinking about thinking") adds to this demand for strong planning if we are to be successful in the classroom. In the last decade alone, we have made large gains in our knowledge of:

> *Multiple intelligences:* Did you know that Dr. Gardner now outlines not seven but eight and a half intelligences? Can you find out how to bring this information into short-range plans?
>
> *Learning styles:* What does it mean to have both "left-brained and right-brained learners" in a class? Do your plans reflect this information?
>
> *Gender differences in learning:* Do boys and girls learn all material in the same way? Can your planning improve equity in the classroom?
>
> *Character education:* Do teachers teach values? You bet. Instruction is never value-free and shouldn't be. Do your plans offer students opportunities to share ideas, learn from different perspectives, and respect differences?

There is much more to consider as teachers plan for curriculum and instruction today. We are interested in:

- Group sizes
- Cooperative learning
- School-to-work transition
- Brain research
- Use of technology
- Attention deficit disorders
- Multiage grouping
- Non-English-speaking children
- Children with special needs in the regular classroom
- Plans devised with other teachers and teams
- Parental involvement in the instructional model
- Experiments with schoolwide units
- Year-round teaching model
- Student interests
- A move beyond textbooks

- Possible national standards, such as "the *National Geography Standards*" or "*NCTM Standards*" (National Council of Teachers of Mathematics)
- More rigorous state guidelines or curriculum "frameworks"
- Integration of disciplines in teaching

How many of these items did you check off? Have you had formal training in any or all of them? Do you wonder how to infuse them, where appropriate, into your planning process? Before you step into a class of bright-eyed four-year-olds, who need to learn their colors, or apathetic fourteen-year-olds, who are struggling with pre-algebra, you must plan the work by drawing on all the information, data, and strategies that are available. There is no one right way to deliver instruction today...not with all we know about learners and learning. Instead, we can design plans that reach out to as many learners in as many ways as we can muster. It is a good idea to commit thirty minutes of planning for every hour of instruction that you deliver...if this is the first time with the content or strategy. Later, you can add to or embellish the lesson. So, don't be shocked when you find planning to be time-consuming. Also, don't be surprised when your time spent in planning yields rich rewards in terms of both student performance and your confidence as a teacher.

Background

In order to understand the impetus to move forward in planning, it is helpful to look *backward* for a moment. Who are some major players in planning? What can we learn from their ideas? Here are a few of my favorites and a brief synopsis of how their contributions helped to shape my views on planning today:

- *John Dewey:* For recognizing the importance of linking new learning to past experiences in a carefully constructed set of "activities" in which youngsters are guided by a caring, facilitating teacher. Dr. Dewey was an *idealist,* the originator of the term *progressive.* Simply put, Dewey believed that children, no matter what their backgrounds, could learn *if they had content-rich, interesting, practical experiences.* Dewey has often gotten bad press in terms of planning. Those educators and parents who staunchly embrace a "back to basics" belief system think that Dewey (and his progressive friends) advocate a loose, free-for-all in the classroom. Not so! To provide the kinds of experiences that Dewey would applaud, teachers must be (1) more than competent in their content preparation and (2) masters of long- and short-range planning. If you want children to have what I term "content in context," then you have to learn to plan and spend time planning.

- *Maria Montessori:* For bringing special needs children into the educational arena and for developing a model for teaching that places the "human tongue" (language) and the "human hand" (activity), both necessary for expression and learning, on common ground. You might not know that Dr. Maria Montessori was a medical doctor, working in Italy. She became an advocate for mentally retarded children. We seldom use that term today, opting for more sensitive descriptors such as challenged or special needs or at risk. That's good. But what's better is Montessori's legacy for *planning for special children.* In both your long-range and short-range plans, consider meaningful ways to include and teach these youngsters. Moreover, Dr. Montessori initiated the use of child-sized furniture in the classroom. That kind of pragmatic thinking is key in planning. How do you plan the physical environment? Will you use worktables or desks? Are centers important to you? Do you want art easels and blocks...even for older children? (I do!) Montessori would urge long-range planners to think about the needs of special children and to consider the physical environment as a teaching tool. To do both of these effectively, long-range planning is critical.

• *William Heard Kilpatrick:* For introducing the "project method," a model that places learning as "part of life," not as a separate endeavor that happens only in schools. Kilpatrick's article "The Project Method," published in the September 1918 issue of *The Teachers College Record* generated requests for *60,000 reprints,* according to curriculum historian Herbert Kliebard. Earlier in the century, the project method was a hot curriculum model. Now, at the dawn of the millennium, the project method is back, only we call it *short-range planning* or *thematic planning.* Fragmented, separate lessons do not deliver a big cognitive punch. Kilpatrick obviously sensed that in his intuitive, creative mind, but in the age of PET scans and MRI scans, we *know* that thematic planning is best. By tracing the heat generated when glucose is injected into the body, cognitive scientists can watch the brain work. When the brain heats up (orange- or yellow-colored scans), a lot of cognitive activity is present. We see that youngsters whose brains are stimulated by music (the Mozart effect) appear to learn more and learn more easily. Pairing learning experiences such as music and mathematics helps children to think and to do. Layering experiences reinforces learning as well, providing different, yet unified experiences.

• *Howard Gardner:* For naming and claiming "multiple intelligences," the theory that explains why each brain is different and that there are many ways in which to learn and to express oneself intelligently. In his pivotal book, *Frames of Mind,* Gardner outlined seven separate intelligences and recently put forth an eighth. How will you plan for linguistic, spatial, musical, scientific, bodily kinesthetic, interpersonal, intrapersonal, and naturalistic kinds of brains?

• *Robert Sylwester:* For making "brain science" more real and accessible to teachers who work with brains on a daily basis. His book, *A Celebration of Neurons,* has become a handbook for teachers who want to think about thinking as they plan for instruction.

• *Sylvia Ashton-Warner:* For using culture and intuition to teach children when other, more traditional methods failed. Ashton-Warner gave planning a less formal, more effective role.

Relying on gut instinct and a genuine desire to make learning valuable and desirable to children are probably your best planning agenda.

Keep in mind that, except for Dr. Kilpatrick, these educators did not write exclusively, or, in some cases, even marginally about planning. Instead, most of them wrote about philosophy, about their successes with students, and about their hopes for schools and for the process of learning. From their ideas and dreams, I have drawn some postulates and paradigms about the art and science of planning. Make no mistake: Good planning involves both art and science.

1 THE ART AND SCIENCE OF PLANNING   **5**

PLANNING AS ART

Planning is art when one considers the course of a year to be a fresh canvas on which a colorful, complex mural of "experiences" will be painted. The faces of individual students and their personalities, cultural differences, genders, interests, and abilities form the texture of the mural. Your intuition, planning skill, garnishing of resources, and creative integration of content make the mural flow and move.

PLANNING AS SCIENCE

Good planning, both in the long term and the short term, also requires deliberate, scientific outlining. There are checkpoints to be covered, observations to be noted, data to be reviewed, and a cruel taskmaster—the calendar—to be reckoned with. Pacing, progress, and accountability measures make planning a science.

In conclusion, planning for long-term goals, as well as planning for the brief daily delivery of lessons, involves elements of both learned skill and natural curiosity. In this book, you can find the tools, if you will, to practice the skills of planning with competency. It is harder, however, to deliver the elements of creativity, balance, curiosity, joy, and caring that are also required for good planning. Knowing how to plan means knowing who you are as teacher, and who you are as a person. Your intelligences—linguistic, musical, kinesthetic, logical, naturalistic—make you either a competent planner or a creative planner. As you gain skill in planning and perhaps develop a more robust interest in planning, your instruction will reflect growth, power, and confidence.

PLANNING AS A SCHOOLWIDE MISSION

There is an ongoing joke among teachers that school folks are operating about "ten years behind" our counterparts in the business world. That might be most accurate in terms of planning. Business and industry saw the importance and value of long-range planning (LRP) more than ten years ago. All MBA candidates worth their power ties could outline the steps in strategic planning, and a change in a corporation's vision statement can drive stock prices up or down! In schools and school districts, planning and the visions or missions that drive planning have become fashionable, but have they become practical? Corporations actually use their plans and the visions that underpin them both to hire and fire and to develop products. Our goal should be to develop long-range plans that truly drive instruction and assessment as well as influence the way that we do business with children. Your school's or district's attitude toward planning is important to consider. Good planning takes time and leadership. If you want to get "all the good out of it" and not turn planning into a meaningless waste of time, then do it right. Here are some suggestions for leaders who are committed to planning:

Planning for Success

- Designate blocks of time at the beginning, middle, and end of the school-year just for planning.

- Provide leadership training for teacher-leaders, not just for administrators.

- Respect individual differences among teachers. If a teacher is successful teaching reading with one model, don't insist upon another model just so your plan is met.

- Create plans that are flexible. For example, make it a goal for teachers to spend sixty minutes of instructional time daily on reading, rather than to use the XYZ Model of Reading exclusively for sixty minutes per day.

- Encourage teachers to attend conferences and workshops; pay for it with your planning funds. Teachers who are excited about their profession and about new ideas become vigorous, energetic planners.

- Become a professional development site (PDS) school in partnership with a local teacher training college. This opportunity brings student teachers and clinical experiences into your school and enables you to help train new teachers who know how to plan right from the beginning. In addition, fresh teacher candidates probably have more experience in long-range and short-range planning than most of your veterans because planning is BIG in teacher education today. These novices can bring planning expertise and energy into your school, and they're free!

- Demonstrate a commitment to planning in your own work. Principals, coordinators, and lead teachers who want teachers to plan well should be practicing the art and science of planning themselves.

- Provide materials, such as software, planning books, and copies of national standards for teachers, so that they don't have to scramble around looking for what they need.

- Bring in consultants and motivational speakers who love planning. Choose these folks carefully. The best strategy is to ask teachers *who they want* to work with.

FIGURE 1.1   Teachers Engaging in a Planning Session

WHY LONG-RANGE PLANNING IS WORTH THE EFFORT _____

During the summer of 1997, I began thinking about the need for a book about planning, especially long-range planning, which has been untouched territory in curriculum theory. I had been piloting an undergraduate course titled *Curriculum and Assessment,* in which future teachers learned how to design long-range plans and actually worked with their cooperating teachers to formulate an LRP for use during their twelve-week student teaching experience. The intern teachers' journals of this experience contained some provoking and sometimes troubling observations:

> "It [long-range planning] is so much harder than I anticipated. How can I see into the future? How will I know what the kids need three months from now?"

> "My cooperating teacher can't share her long-range plans with me to help me get started. She says that they just take it day by day. Now what do I do?"

> "Planning for the long term makes me think really hard. I have to decide how units will flow and which skills to put together with other skills. It is hard doing this, but I can't imagine *not doing this."*

> "I'm excited about my long-range plan. It is probably my best work in college because nobody told me what to do. I made it happen."

> "The teachers in my team [at the school] are worried about doing long-range plans now and want to see my class notes. It [long-range planning] is part of their evaluation now, and they [the teachers] didn't learn how to do this in college."

Fascinated by this slice of life cut from the students' journals, I wanted a bigger perspective. Turning to the Internet, I posed a few questions about long-range planning to teachers in the United States and Canada, using the vehicle of a teacher's chat room. Within hours, passionate replies poured in from cyberspace:

> "Long-range planning…who are you kidding? They [administration] want us to do it, but we have no time to work together. Sure, I feel that I *need to do it,* but when?"

> "I don't need to put a long-range plan on paper. It is in my head."

> "Thank goodness somebody is talking about long-range planning. It suddenly appeared on our evaluation for tenure and merit pay, and we don't know how to do it."

> "It [long-range planning] is a lot of work. What are they [plans] supposed to look like? I don't have a clue."

> "We're going to have to do long-range planning, especially with inclusion and all these kids with different learning styles. You can't do the right things unless you plan ahead."

Long-range planning is here. But are teachers prepared to deal with it? Like any new challenge, attitude is everything. If you want to be successful in long-range planning, then you must be convinced that it is worth your time and effort. Here are some reasons to invest in an LRP:

- You will save time in the long run because materials and resources will be ordered ahead of time.

- You can design the classroom to meet the needs of children and won't waste time rearranging.

- You will be able to preplan groups and projects because you will have an awareness of achievement levels.

- You can share units and speakers with other teachers because you know when things will be happening.

- You will be more relaxed and prepared because you have set up the curriculum for success.

- You will design and carry out more meaningful, valid assessment of student learning because your content will be measured out and organized. This will result in better student performance.

- You will be prepared for your own evaluation, which will probably require a demonstration of your ability to do long-range planning.

Long-range planning is both a process and a product. Whether one is a novice teacher or an expert in the field, long-range planning challenges our expectations for teaching and learning. It is inevitable because each LRP is unique, reflecting the composition of the student group, the current curriculum objectives, the worldviews of parents, and the personality of the teacher.

LOOKING AHEAD TO CHAPTER TWO

In the next chapter, we will walk through the steps for long-range planning and inspect a model for designing your own plan. Like Christy, the young teacher in Catherine Marshall's book, the reality of making a plan work for children can be daunting. It can help to see a "good plan" before embarking on your own task.

Allow yourself the luxury of reading a novel about a teacher whom you admire. This might be fiction or nonfiction. Consider how personal style affects planning. Here are some choices to consider:
✓ *Teacher,* Sylvia Ashton-Warner
✓ *To Teach: The Journey of a Teacher,* William Ayers
✓ *The Saber-Tooth Curriculum,* Harold Benjamin
✓ *Brighten the Corner Where You Are,* Fred Chappell
✓ *Marva Collins's Way,* Marva Collins
✓ *The Water Is Wide,* Pat Conroy
✓ *Experience and Education,* John Dewey
✓ *How Children Learn,* John Holt
✓ *My Posse Don't Do Homework,* LouAnne Johnston
✓ *The Dead Poet's Society,* N. H. Kleinbau
✓ *Schoolteacher: A Sociological Study,* Dan Lortie
✓ *Christy,* Catherine Marshall

CHAPTER 2

Designing Long-Range Plans

*Yet I sincerely needed a working philosophy on which to
hang my hat. After the Halloween trip, one began to form
and crystallize without my knowledge, and when I finally
acknowledged its presence, it was already a part of me:
simply that life was good, but it was hard; we would prepare
to meet it head on, but we would enjoy the preparation.*

(Pat Conroy, writing in *The Water Is Wide,* concerning his long-term goals for the
children whom he taught on the isolated South Carolina barrier island, Yamacraw)

Like Pat Conroy, who was untrained as a teacher when he accepted the challenge of teaching on an island accessible only by boat, many teachers feel lost when it comes to designing long-range plans. We know that we need them. We have a general idea of what we want floating in our heads, but the actual task of putting an LRP down on paper can seem daunting. This chapter can help you overcome your concerns about LRPs, and there is a model plan designed by one of my students, who used the techniques that I will outline in this section. Students often plead with teachers, "Show us what it is supposed to be." So there is a sample included to satisfy your curiosity!

Every long-range plan, whether for pre-K music or ninth-grade algebra, will have two distinct parts: the narrative and the schedule.

THE NARRATIVE: THE FIRST COMPONENT OF AN LRP

In the narrative, one sets the stage for the curriculum map laid out in the schedule. The narrative contains the following information:

- A description of the student group

- A discussion of special needs of the student group

- A set of goals for the year (academic/behavioral/affective)

- A listing of sources for verification of the goals

- A rationale statement of your personal philosophy and agenda concerning the year ahead

- A plan for communicating with parents

- A plan for assessing student work

- A design for managing your classroom

- A plan for managing student behavior and learning

- An explanation of how you will identify and secure resources, materials, and technology to support the instructional units described in the following section (schedule)

- Attachments of documents and forms that support the information listed above

How to Get Started

The first step in designing a long-range plan is to review *what you are supposed to be teaching* in this grade level or this area of the curriculum. Now, that may seem strange when the first section of the LRP is defined as a description of the students. Why don't you consider the students first?

Your job is to present the curriculum in a way that is meaningful to the students. To that end, you must know the curriculum very well. Remember, an LRP is *individualized*, not personalized. There's a distinct difference.

No human being, no matter how competent, organized, or talented, can personalize a regular classroom: You cannot meet the needs of every student. In educational circles, we like to say we can, but it is empty jargon as far as I am concerned.

However, you can do a credible job of *individualizing* the curriculum, that is, making it quite likely that the *students will get it,* if you spend some time up front designing a good LRP.

Following is a checklist of materials that you might gather in order to do a thorough review of what you are supposed to be teaching.

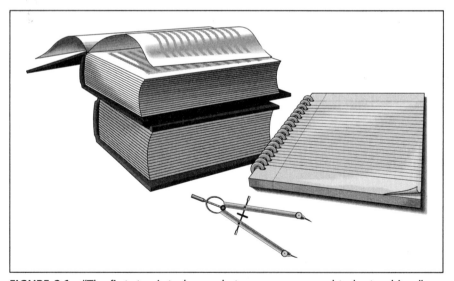

FIGURE 2.1   "The first step is to *know* what you are supposed to be teaching."

FIGURE 2.2 Checklist for Curriculum Review

Item	Source	Notes
National standards for your field		
State standards, guidelines, and frameworks		
District-level objectives for the grade or subject		
Textbooks with scope and sequence charts		
Units and course syllabi		
Novels and children's literature		
Standardized test information		

In addition to the checklist offered above, it is valuable to sit down with a team of experienced teachers, if you are a novice, to *find out what you are supposed to be teaching*. If you are a master teacher already, it is helpful to sit down with a group of colleagues to explore the question: *How can we teach the curriculum in a better way?*

Thinking Hint: *Experienced teachers should mentor novice teachers in the design of long-range plans. The 1997 National Commission on Teaching and America's Future found that elementary teachers have only 8.3 minutes of preparatory time for every hour they teach. How can you make the most of that time or work to secure more time for planning?*

Notice, too, that there is a continuum of curriculum sources, moving from:

National Standards

State Guidelines and Frameworks

District-Level Curriculum Objectives

Textbook Scope and Sequence

Preferred or Individualized Materials
(Test Data, Books, Novels, Units of Study, Syllabi)

FIGURE 2.3   Write your ideas in the bubble.

FIGURE 2.4 Curriculum Connections

Complete this Curriculum Connections worksheet to help you begin to focus on the main concepts that you want to include in your LRP.

The 10 Most Important Concepts to Include in My LRP

1.   6.

2.   7.

3.   8.

4.   9.

5.   10.

Now that you have reviewed the curriculum, it is time to consider the *who* factor. Who are the students you will teach? You can use the following sources to help in your investigation of the description of students:

✓ Permanent student records

✓ Parent interviews

✓ Teacher recommendations

✓ Individualized education plans (IEPs) and individualized transition plans (ITPs)

✓ Psychological test results

✓ Personality inventories

✓ Portfolios of student work

✓ Anecdotal records

✓ Grade books

✓ Writing samples

✓ Data from guidance office

What you are looking for are the following:

• Demographics such as gender, ethnicity, age, free or reduced lunch status, and primary culture and/or religion (if it impacts schooling)

• Family information such as single-parent family, illness in family, separation, divorce, or death of parent

• Ability information such as repeating a grade, placement in a gifted program, or referral for special services

• The existence of an IEP, ITP, or 504 plan

• Special needs such as diabetes, allergies, or hearing aids

• Progress in the curriculum (on grade level, above grade level, or below grade level)

• IQ or multiple intelligence test reports

• Learning styles as evidenced by anecdotal records or examples of work

• Reading level

• Completion of district-level objectives

• Primary language/secondary language

• Diagnosis of attention deficit disorder (ADD) or other learning impairment

• Student interests and motivation to learn

Thinking Hint: *Keep in mind that the collection of these data is considered private and confidential. It is* for your eyes only, *to be used for the purpose of shaping the curriculum to a more individualized set of concepts and instruction.*

Sensitive information, such as gender and ethnicity, can be helpful if one believes, as I do, that gender and ethnicity can impact the ways that students prefer to learn. In my book More Than Pink and Blue: How Gender Shapes Your

Curriculum, *I present applications of current brain research on how boys and girls might learn differently. Girls, for example, often prefer to do math in groups rather than individually. Ethnicity can influence learning preference, too. In certain Asian cultures, for example, youngsters are hesitant about making eye contact with an adult or answering boldly. If your classroom is too unstructured, these youngsters can feel out of place or feel that they are being asked to be disrespectful to you, the teacher. The clue is to find out as much as you can about the different ethnic and cultural groups represented in your class.*

Next, you will find a grid that you can fill in with your own criteria to help organize the search for student information that will feed into the LRP.

Answer the following question in this space:

"What do I expect to learn from this description of students that might shape the way that this schoolyear unfolds?"

FIGURE 2.5

FIGURE 2.6 Student Information Grid

Teacher _____ Schoolyear _____

Grade Level or Subject Area _____ School _____

Insert your data in this grid. Use the numbers to identify your criteria:
1 = age, 2 = gender, etc.

Name	1	2	3	4	5	6	7	8	9	10	Notes

Now, using these data, write a section in which you "think out loud" about how you might set up your classroom and structure the schedule that will follow to meet the needs of your students. Here are some prompts to help you get started:

✓ What did I learn about the cultural backgrounds of my students that might shape the LRP?

✓ Are there any family problems that might impact the class?

✓ Will I need to make changes in the physical environment?

✓ What are the ranges of ability groups? Will this affect pacing?

✓ How did the students' achievement tests look? Will I need to do a lot of review, or can I move on?

✓ Are there any troubled students who might benefit from a behavioral contract?

✓ Did examples of student work hint at learning styles?

✓ Did I locate any "repeaters," slow learners, or gifted students who might need special plans?

✓ Are there IEPs or ITPs to consider?

✓ How can I structure units that make the most of what I've learned from the description of students?

✓ Should I prepare for a student with an attention problem?

✓ Does every child speak English as the primary language?

✓ Do I need more information about specific students before moving on with the LRP design?

✓ Will I need to consider "pull-out" disruptions for students who go out for speech therapy or occupational therapy (OT)?

Notes on student descriptions (include how these data impact my overall LRP)

_____

_____

_____

_____

_____

_____

_____

_____

_____

_____

It isn't enough to rely on what you *already know.* Find out current data as soon as you can. Send notes home. Do home visits. Do what it takes to get to know your students. Getting to know your students as quickly as possible, using a variety of instruments and interviews, is the *best way* to shape an LRP.

Use a student interest inventory or a questionnaire to accomplish this. In the sample LRPs, you will see how teachers plan to understand their students.

The Next Step: Writing Goals for the Year

After assessing your students, you are ready to set goals:

1. You will need three kinds of goals: academic, behavioral, and affective.

2. Goals are broad statements about *what you expect students to know and be able to do* by the end of the year.

3. You should feel accountable for students meeting those goals.

4. Goals will feed *directly into curriculum objectives in the schedule and in the short-range and daily plans.*

5. You can create your own goals OR select them from the national, state, or local standards described earlier in the chapter on page 11.

6. It is helpful and wise for teams of teachers to agree on goals for the year, so that you can work together and so that parents are not confused.

Academic Goals

❑ Two or three academic goals for each subject area

❑ Two or three academic goals for each major concept

❑ Matched to standards

❑ Open enough to accommodate ability differences

Examples

❑ Students will read and comprehend materials on grade level.

❑ Students will apply proper grammar and spelling skills in writing tasks.

❑ Students will demonstrate problem-solving skills in fourth-grade mathematics.

❑ Students will complete the tenth-grade objectives for AP biology.

How do you want students to conduct themselves in your classroom? What kinds of learning skills do you want them to demonstrate on a daily basis? These questions feed into your behavioral goals.

Behavioral Goals

❑ Two or three behavioral goals per LRP

❑ Broad enough to cover the variety of skill and ability levels

❑ Keeping cultural and gender differences in mind

Examples

❑ Students will use questioning and research skills to complete their work.

❑ Students will learn to work independently and in cooperative groups.

❑ Students will follow the classroom and school rules to ensure a safe learning environment.

❑ Students will use laboratory materials appropriately and safely.

Be careful with this next section. Your goal is not to be a "social engineer" but to help children learn to respect their own gifts and talents, and those of others, while promoting a safe learning environment.

Affective Goals

❑ Two or three affective goals per LRP

❑ Carefully worded to avoid offending parents or treading too far into spiritual territory that belongs to family and church

Examples

❑ Students will recognize their unique gifts and use them in learning.

❑ Students will have opportunities to speak freely and to share their feelings in a safe environment.

❑ Students will demonstrate caring and kindness toward classmates.

Notes for Writing Goals for the LRP

_____

_____

_____

_____

_____

_____

_____

Thinking Hint: *After designing your goals, invite students to ADD one more goal for each area: academic, behavioral, and affective. Teach your students to take responsibility for their own learning and growth by learning to write and pursue long-term goals.*

Begin a draft of your LRP goals here:

Academic Goals

1. _____

2. _____

3. _____

4. _____

5. _____

6. _____

Behavioral Goals

1. _____

2. _____

3. _____

Affective Goals

1. _____

2. _____

3. _____

Sources of Verification

The LRP doesn't simply exist…it had parents. The parents of the LRP are standards and objectives. The relatives of the LRP are books, novels, test data, and supporting content material. I ask my students at the university: "Who told you to teach this?" That is the question you must answer to justify your LRP. Prepare a verification list or statement that *documents your sources* for the schedule of units and lessons that will follow:

Examples

The National Geography Standards

The National Social Studies Standards

Exploring Our World through Geography (third-grade edition)

State Frameworks for Social Studies

My District's Geography Concept Checklist

Thinking Hint: *Ask yourself, as you look through these documents, "Who says I'm supposed to be teaching these concepts, and why are they important?" That is the process of verification. It is not just about* checking up *on sources; it is about* checking out *your sources.*

Use this form to list the sources of verification for your LRP.

Name of Source	National	State	Local	Preferred/Personal
_____				_____
_____				_____
_____				_____
_____				_____
_____				_____
_____				_____
_____				_____

Thinking Hint: *Ask yourself the following questions:*

✓ Are these sources current?

✓ Have I spent time with these sources and do I feel sure that the content is valid and acceptable?

✓ Do I have a variety of verification sources?

✓ Are these sources approved by the school district?

✓ Have I cited titles, authors, and publication dates for the sources?

✓ Can I also use these sources in short-range plan design?

✓ Do I have my own copy of each resource in case an evaluation team or parent wants to check them out?

✓ Can I explain WHY I chose each source for planning?

✓ What are my questions or concerns about verification?

Let's review. So far, you have:

- Reviewed the curriculum.

- Investigated and analyzed your student group.

- Verified your sources for content.

- Pulled academic, behavioral, and affective goals for the year from your sources.

Now you need to:

- Formulate a rationale statement for the LRP.

The rationale statement is your *personal investment and analysis* of what will appear in the schedule. You analyze, summarize, and evaluate the standards and mix them with your description of student group information and generally talk about HOW and WHY you will set up the classroom and corresponding instruction. I tell my students to imagine that they are having a cup of coffee with a friend and simply telling about their exciting plans for the schoolyear. A rationale statement is akin to a personal "mission plan" for teachers:

Tips for Writing a Rationale Statement

❏ Make it one to two pages in length.

❏ Avoid educational jargon.

❏ Set the stage for what observers might see and students might experience in your classroom.

The purpose of the rationale statement is to "pull your thoughts together" before you embark on the schedule of units and lessons. Below are some prompts for beginning rationale statements:

- My classroom will...

- If you were to visit my algebra class, you would see...

- To meet the needs of my students, I will...

- My rationale for using children's literature in every unit is...

- Science process skills are really important to my teaching so...

- If you were to visit...

- Every day we will...

- It is important for children to...

- I believe in...

- This year, we will try to...

- What's special about my LRP is...

- I plan to…
- To help the students become competent writers, we will…
- With so many visual learners in the group, we will…
- Thinking skills are critical so…
- My personal teaching style is…

Use this space to write a draft of your LRP rationale statement. Try one of the prompts from pages 23–24 to get you started!

Draft of Your Rationale Statement

_____

_____

_____

_____

_____

_____

_____

_____

_____

_____

_____

_____

_____

_____

_____

_____

_____

_____

_____

_____

_____

_____

_____

_____

_____

_____

_____

_____

_____

_____

_____

_____

_____

_____

_____

_____

_____

_____

Your Plan for Assessment

It is important to *plan for assessment* in the LRP. This section helps you to accomplish four important tasks in teaching:

✓ To think about what you expect students to know when the instruction is complete.

✓ To think about what you expect students to be able to do when the instruction is complete.

✓ To set up both traditional and authentic assessment plans.

✓ To set up a practical record-keeping system to keep up with student progress.

Getting started: Respond to the following questions to formulate a one-page assessment plan:

⟹ How often will I do assessment?

_____

_____

_____

⟹ Will I only use traditional assessment, such as chapter tests and quizzes, or will I also use portfolios or work sampling?

_____

_____

_____

⟹ What kind of record-keeping system will I use for assessment? Grade book? Rubrics and checklists? Reports? Charts?

_____

_____

_____

⟹ Is there a plan for informing students of their progress? Parents?

_____

_____

_____

_____

⟹ Will all assessments be formal and graded, or will there be more frequent, informal checkpoints?

_____

_____

_____

⟹ Do I plan to do only individual assessment, or will there be group projects or cooperative tasks that require a different kind of assessment?

_____

_____

_____

⇨ Am I preparing students for national and state-level achievement tests? How will this test preparation fit into my long-range plan for assessment?

_____

_____

_____

⇨ Using my description of students, are there special needs for assessment, such as nonreaders, English-as-a-second-language (ESL) youngsters, deaf children, or those whose 504 plans mandate accommodations for assessment? How will I do this in a meaningful, practical way?

_____

_____

_____

⇨ Will technology play a role in my assessment plan? For example, will I use something like *Accelerated Reader* to keep up with student progress in reading, or even a computer program for record keeping?

_____

_____

_____

Notes on Assessment:

_____

_____

_____

_____

Parent Communication and the LRP

Parent communication that really works begins with the LRP because you are making an earnest, sincere commitment to it, before the year even begins! If you desire real, ongoing parent communication, then build it into your LRP. It is a good idea to offer an example of communication with parents if you are a student teacher or if your LRP is being evaluated for tenure, promotion, or merit pay. Here are some ideas for parent communication that you can describe and, if you like, attach as examples to the LRP:

Parent Communication Ideas

- Parent newsletters (try personalizing them by using your name: *Mrs. Bone's Bulletin*)
- Envelopes of work that go home on a specific day of the week
- Parent communication postcards

- E-mail newsletters
- A Web site with class information
- A homework hotline for the telephone
- Inserts in report cards

Outline your personalized plan for parent communication in the space below:

_____

_____

_____

_____

_____

In the LRP, you must also lay out your plan for incorporating outside resources, innovative materials, and technology into the schedule of units and lessons that will be more *specific*. For example, if you plan to use a VCR and monitor frequently, how will you access that technology? Do you need to order films or laser disks such as *Windows on Science*? What about setting up field trips and speakers? Will you need special lab equipment? This section should be closely aligned with your rationale statement. Here's an example: If you said in your rationale statement that writing a class newsletter would be an integral part of your language arts and social studies curricula and you don't have adequate computer resources in the classroom, *then you will need to schedule time twice a week in the school's computer lab.*

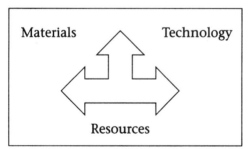

FIGURE 2.7

Use this section to brainstorm necessary materials, resources, and technology that will enable you to implement your schedule of instruction seamlessly and smoothly:

Field Trips

❑ _____

❑ _____

❑ _____

Speakers

❑ _____

❑ _____

❑ _____

❑ _____

❑ _____

Technology

❑ _____

❑ _____

❑ _____

❑ _____

❑ _____

❑ _____

Equipment

❑ _____

❑ _____

❑ _____

❑ _____

Computer Lab or Science Lab Time

❑ _____

❑ _____

❑ _____

❑ _____

Books and Authentic Materials from Outside Sources

❑ _____

❑ _____

❑ _____

❑ _____

Internet Access, Software, and Laser Disks

❑ _____

❑ _____

❑ _____

❑ _____

Accommodations for Furniture or Equipment for Special Needs

❑ _____

❑ _____

❑ _____

Magazines, Periodicals, and Films

❑ _____

❑ _____

❑ _____

Art Materials and Background Music

❑ _____

❑ _____

❑ _____

(continued)

(Continued)

*Models, Manipulatives, and Materials
for Math and Science*

❑ _____

❑ _____

❑ _____

❑ _____

*Publishing Center Materials
and Equipment*

❑ _____

❑ _____

❑ _____

*Research Materials, Dictionaries,
Thesauri, and Atlases*

❑ _____

❑ _____

❑ _____

Equipment for Gross and Fine Motor Skills

❑ _____

❑ _____

❑ _____

Routine Classroom Supplies

❑ _____

❑ _____

❑ _____

Classroom Rule #1: Follow the LRP _____

One of the final components of the narrative section of the LRP is the description of your classroom management plan and a set of classroom rules. Although this plan may be refined as you move into the schoolyear, it is important to *plan ahead for how you will deal with behavior and routine activities.* Much of the new and most provocative research on classroom management suggests that it is a lack of planning and a strict adherence to the rules and procedures of the classroom that result in poor student behavior and loss of instructional time.

It is not the purpose of this book to teach you how to develop a classroom management plan. Suffice it to say that a concise, pragmatic version of a management plan is part of the narrative section of the LRP.

However, here are a few benchmarks of solid management plans to help you evaluate the potential of your document:

- Procedures for fire and storm drills

- Procedures for dealing with hostile intruders and violence

- Procedures for collecting homework, book money, and lunch money

- A concise set of classroom rules and expectations

- Consequences for breaking classroom rules

- Plans for managing transition times

- A description of your reward system

THE SCHEDULE: THE SECOND COMPONENT OF AN LRP _____

The second, and some might say easier, part of the long-range plan is the schedule. In the schedule are the following:

- Major concepts, chapters, skills, and units

- The sequence and order for these concepts, chapters, skills, and units

- The estimated pacing of these concepts, chapters, skills, and units

- Approximate dates and types of assessment of these concepts, chapters, skills, and units

- Target dates for parent communication

- Target dates for field trips, speakers, and events

- The timeline for your curriculum

The schedule keeps you on task and accountable.

One observant intern teacher at the university remarked, "The narrative is like keeping a journal, and the schedule is like keeping a diary." That's rather profound and, I think, accurate.

What Does a Schedule Look Like? _____

The schedule can take many forms and should be as practical and easy to manipulate as you can make it. It is meant to be a *work in progress*. Here are some formats for the scheduling component of an LRP that I have seen interns and teachers use with success:

- A blank monthly calendar

- A timeline with phases, units, and dates marked on it

- A chart or poster paper with colored stickers to key in data (hung on the wall)

- A document created on a computer, using symbols and text (similar to a formal course syllabus)

- A course syllabus

- Color-coded sheets to represent subject areas, pulled together in a three-ring binder

- A file on a computer disk, accessed by your personal laptop

- A "daytimer" or date book (large) filled in with pencil

- Planning forms held on a clipboard (to hang in the classroom)

Schedule Checklist

✓ You demonstrate enough detail about the content that you will cover to enable you, the administration, and parents to know how much and what kind of material will be covered during a period of time.

✓ Your personal style can be emphasized in the way you set up and fill in the schedule.

✓ The schedule should be specific in terms of content.

✓ It is not a bad idea to list skills or objectives on the schedule.

✓ The schedule should flow out of the long-term goals that you set forth in the narrative.

✓ It is helpful to select statements for the schedule directly from standards or curriculum objectives.

Here are some examples of what you might see in a schedule:

Begin unit on fractions
Chapter 3. Two weeks.
Set up pizza party for end of unit.

Study of WW II continues.
Speaker on Holocaust.
Interim reports due.
Order films for next unit from state dept.

Grammar checkpoint on punctuation in business and friendly letters.
Field trip to post office.

FIGURE 2.8

Thinking Hint: *Practice writing a few schedule notes in the scrolls on this page.*

Use enough detail to satisfy your own level of organization.

Make your schedule notes practical, clear, and easy to follow. Think of them as markers on a road map.

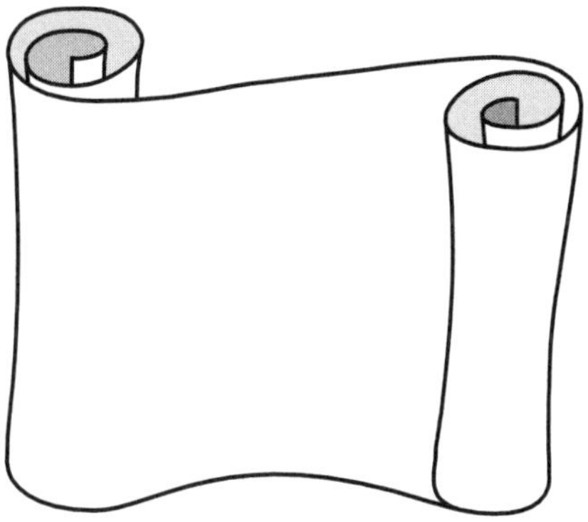

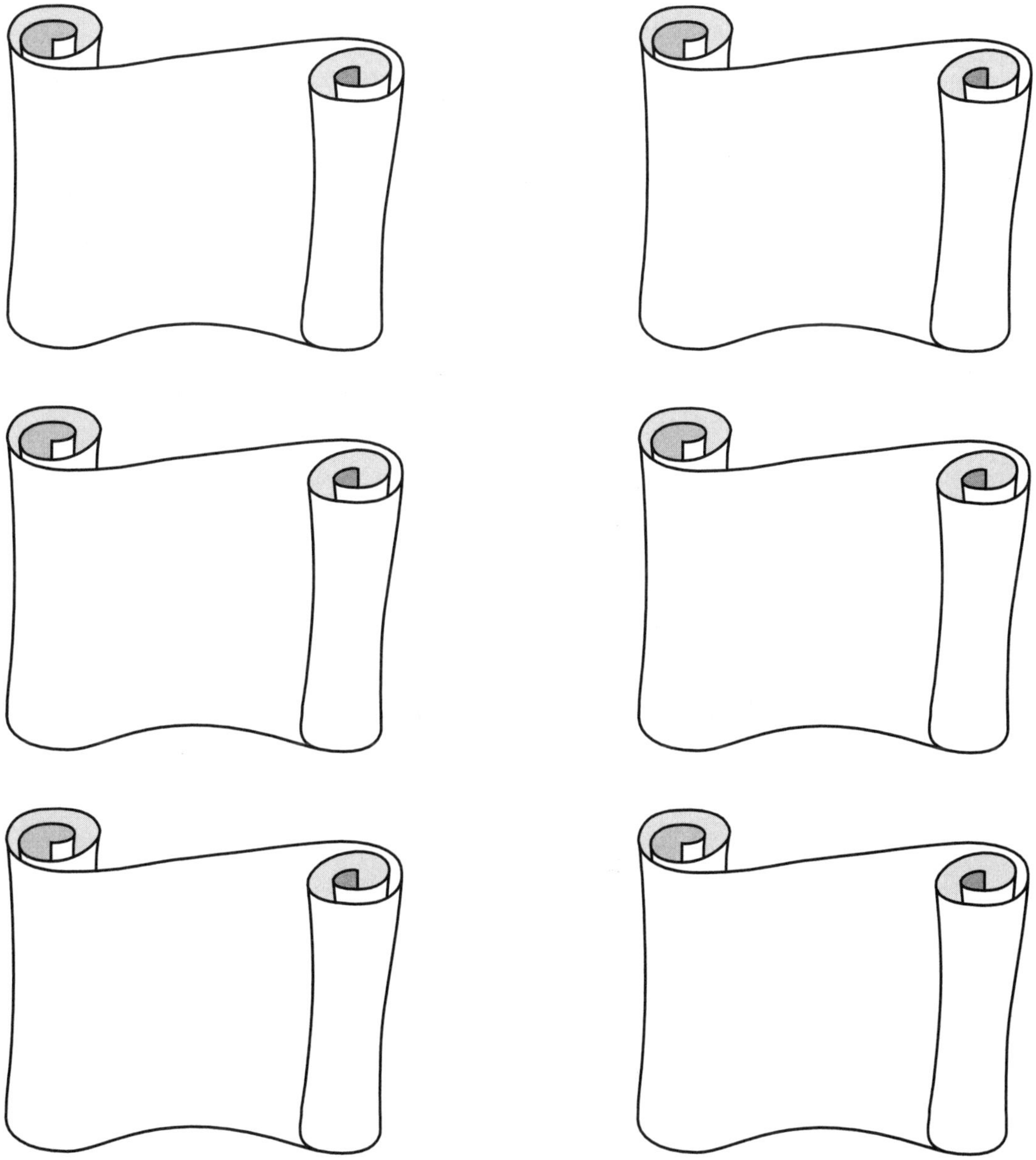

When you create your schedule, here are some suggestions:

Organizational Tips for Creating Your Schedule

✓ Use themes to keep the schedule flowing.

✓ Chapter titles can be good benchmarks.

✓ Use the schedule as an opportunity for teaching compatible material or concepts, such as a chapter on weather in science and a unit on measurement (heat, temperature, rainfall) in mathematics.

✓ Consider children's books or novels as unifying elements in a schedule.

✓ Make sure that you don't overload the students with too many assessments at one time when you set out the year.

✓ It is okay to plan a block of nine weeks or one semester at a time when you are starting out. A year can be too much for a novice!

✓ Work with team members or mentor teachers to design a schedule that is workable and not too ambitious.

✓ Check your schedule against testing requirements and standards. Will you cover critical concepts before children are tested on them?

✓ Figure holidays and seasonal celebrations into the schedule design.

✓ Be careful with pacing. Most long-range planners push too much content into a schedule and do not teach for *mastery*. It is no good if the children don't know the material.

Think of the schedule as your personal *map of the year.* Where do you want the students to start? What landmarks will they need to visit? How far will you travel each week? Will there be resting points? How will you evaluate the success of the trip...and when?

Thinking Hint: *Use these pages to practice writing a schedule of several weeks for your LRP. Reproduce these pages, if you like, and make them into a schedule booklet.*

FIGURE 2.9 Schedule Form for the LRP

Week of _____ Class or Subject _____

Concepts or skills

Pacing

Special considerations

Ordering materials

Assessment

Week of _____ Class or Subject _____

Concepts or skills

Pacing

Special considerations

Ordering materials

Assessment

Week of _____ Class or Subject _____

Concepts or skills

Pacing

Special considerations

Ordering materials

Assessment

(continued)

FIGURE 2.9   continued

Theme or unit of study _____ Time frame _____

Objectives covered

Special considerations

Activities

Integration with other subjects

Assessment

_____

Theme or unit of study _____ Time frame _____

Objectives covered

Special considerations

Activities

Integration with other subjects

Assessment

_____

Theme or unit of study _____ Time frame _____

Objectives covered

Special considerations

Activities

Integration with other subject

Assessment

_____

Notes for the Theme or Unit Study

❑ _____

❑ _____

❑ _____

WRAPPING UP THE LONG-RANGE PLAN

Long-range planning is part art and part science. It is also a personal statement that draws on a teacher's preferences and style in the classroom. One of the joys of long-range planning is the opportunity to share your passion for a content area, for children's books, for writing, or for research with your students.

When a reviewer or parent looks at your LRP, what is the overall impression? One way to build excitement for long-range planning is to establish your personal LRP imprint:

- Technology-Talented: Students will be using the Internet and computers, and maybe even creating a Web site!

- The Write Stuff: Students are writing all the time!

- Skill-Centered: Your aim is to teach mastery of basic skills!

- Leaning toward Literature: Students will be immersed in reading novel after novel, and your content will be woven into and among themes drawn from great books!

- Integration of Everything: Chapters and units match up neatly to build on one another and on common themes!

- Science- or Social Studies-Centered: You make experiments or continents the jumping-off place for lots of other learning!

- Thinking Skills-Centered: Your lessons are built around higher-order thinking skills and problem solving instead of sequenced skills!

- Moved by Mathematics: Major math themes move your program along, with science, social studies, and even language drawn into the calculation!

Before we look at two sample long-range plans, think about this bit of encouragement: LRPs are meant to be changed. By the end of the schoolyear, the LRP should be dog-eared and coffee-stained. So, while you should plan it seriously, don't take it *too* seriously. Always write your LRP in pencil.

Notes for Long-Range Planning

_____

_____

_____

_____

_____

LOOKING AHEAD TO CHAPTER THREE

The teacher has an additional handicap in maintaining attention: unlike the director of a play, the teacher has little "artistic control" over the enterprise. Teachers cannot select or reject scripts; they frequently must follow curricula which bore students or are beyond their capacities.
(Dan Lortie writing in *Schoolteacher,* a sociological study of the profession)

Checklists for analyzing the sample LRPs are provided to help you approach the task in a more organized manner. An LRP is a lengthy document. Therefore, only part of each schedule is included so that two samples can be reviewed. Here are the checklists:

Elementary Plan
✓ Note the detail in the description of students (page 42).
✓ Note the personal beliefs woven into the rationale statement (pages 43–44).
✓ Note how this teacher emphasizes units of instruction and gives suggested duration for the units.
✓ Note how this teacher gives specific concepts to be covered in her schedule.

Sample Plan for the Primary Grades
✓ Note how the primary plan is built around kindergarten objectives rather than concept-driven units.
✓ Note how this teacher's materials list is shown separately. This is a matter of preference.
✓ Note that this primary plan is more simple and concise, since the goal of kindergarten is to prepare and socialize, whereas the fifth-grade teacher must cover five different academic areas in detail.

Overall Notes
✓ Length of the plan becomes part of your personal style. Both teachers covered all the requisite parts of the LRP, but they gave only the details that they felt compelled to share.
✓ Though addenda are mentioned in the plans, such as anecdotal note sheets, parent newsletters, and interest inventories, they are not included in this book for reasons of editing and length. It is nice, however, to include them in your personal plan.
✓ Many school districts will provide their own expectations for long-range planning. Keep in mind, however, that the guidelines in this chapter will help you to formulate the basis of almost any kind of LRP.

Sample Long-Range Plans—Elementary and Primary

*Having set up an educational goal, New-Fist proceeded to
construct a curriculum for reaching that goal. "What things must
we tribesmen know how to do in order to live with full bellies,
warm backs, and minds free from fear?" he asked himself.*

(New-Fist, the first teacher pondering the design of the first LRP, in *The Saber-Tooth
Curriculum,* a parody about teaching and curriculum design, by Harold Benjamin)

Two sample long-range plans are found in Chapter Three. They were designed
by intern teachers who followed the guidelines provided in Chapters One and
Two. Notice the degree of detail and critical thinking demonstrated by these
teachers. They showcase not only the curriculum but the reasons for teaching
and methods for instructing in that curriculum. A word to consider as you
analyze these LRPs is *metacognition,* or "thinking about thinking." In LRP
design, the teacher attempts to get inside the minds of students in order to
plan for elements of content, relevance, and timing.

SAMPLE ELEMENTARY LONG-RANGE PLAN

I. Description of Students

In my fifth-grade class at Anywhere Elementary School, I am responsible for teaching all core subjects, including Language Arts, Math, Science, and Social Studies. Health is considered a part of the science curriculum. Although my students attend Art and Music classes as part of special area instruction, I also strive to integrate the creative arts into core subjects in the regular classroom.

My homeroom consists of twenty-four students. There are eleven girls (six black, four white, one Asian American) and thirteen boys (seven black, five white, one Hispanic). Ages range from ten to twelve. Eleven of these children qualify for free or reduced lunch. Two students receive resource assistance for math and reading; one of these students also receives speech therapy. Three students are in the gifted program (ACE), but eight students are working at low academic levels. Six students have been diagnosed with attention deficit disorder, for which they take medication. The most recent BSAP test scores for these students indicated that 42 percent were below the 50 percent national percentile in reading, and 28 percent were below the 50 percent national percentile in math.

Since my classroom consists of children working at both low and high academic levels, I will assess and adjust my lessons to meet the needs of all students. All lessons will include enrichment activities designed to keep high achievers motivated and remediation time for those working at lower levels. Information gathered during the first week of school on Personal Profile Sheets and Learning Style Assessment/Student Interest Surveys (attachments A and B) indicates that nine students are visual learners, five are auditory learners, and ten are tactile learners. Analysis of these data helps me ensure that the learning styles of students will be taken into consideration as I plan lessons and projects to accommodate their needs. I will strive to create lessons that include work at various levels of Bloom's taxonomy.

II. Long-Range Goals for Students

Affective Goals:
1. Students will interact respectfully with one another while working alone, in cooperative groups, or in whole-group settings.
2. Students will develop self-control and self-discipline.
3. Students will develop a respect for knowledge and will take responsibility for their own learning.

Academic Goals for Language Arts:
1. Students will critically analyze and evaluate language.
2. Students will use personal experience, the printed word, and information gained from observation as a basis for constructing meaning.
3. Students will use language processes and strategies effectively to communicate in a variety of ways.

Academic Goals for Math:
1. Students will learn mathematics in familiar, realistic contexts having connection to other mathematics or to other disciplines.
2. Students will learn mathematics with understanding in order to make sense of things.
3. Students will take responsibility for their own learning and understanding of mathematics.
4. Students will learn mathematics in order to help them in solving real-life problems.

Academic Goals for Science:
1. Students will learn scientific concepts through active involvement and will use the science process skills.
2. Students will learn science by relating instructional experiences to everyday life.
3. Students will learn about science by talking, writing, and communicating.

Academic Goals for Social Studies:
1. Students will use maps and globes to analyze and understand geographic relationships.
2. Students will be familiar with current events that influence societies throughout the world.
3. Students will understand environmental and ecological concepts that affect human systems globally.
4. Students will understand the factors that have influenced the history of the United States.

Academic Goals for Health:
1. Students will develop an understanding of their own feelings and the feelings of others.
2. Students will develop an understanding of the importance of personal health.
3. Students will develop an understanding of the health habits that can help protect us from disease.

Academic Goals for Creative Arts:
1. Students will develop an appreciation for the arts.
2. Students will use the creative arts as a means of expression.
3. Students will learn the aesthetic value of creative arts.

III. Rationale

Goals and objectives for these long-range plans are derived from standards outlined in the *Charleston County Curriculum Guides* for grade 5, as well as the *National Geography Standards* and appropriate textbooks. The *South Carolina English Language Arts Framework* (grades 4–5), the *South Carolina Mathematics Framework* (grades 3–6), the *South Carolina Visual and Performing Arts Framework* (grades 3–5), and the *South Carolina Science Framework* (grades 3–6) are also used as the basis for these objectives. Although adherence to the standards set forth in these guidelines is my goal, it is understood that plans may be adjusted at any time to accommodate the needs of students.

In the area of Language Arts, students will be taught reading, language, and spelling in a manner that focuses on the real-life relevance of those skills. Students will see how subjects are tied to one another with the use of journals, and they will use language arts skills as a means for communicating in various ways.

Mathematics instruction will include the use of manipulatives, as well as hands-on activities, that will aid in the comprehension of mathematical concepts appropriate at the fifth-grade level. Problem-solving skills will be emphasized. Students will apply mathematical concepts to real-life situations for better understanding.

Social Studies instruction will focus on understanding both current events and those of historical importance. Various resources will be used to enhance classroom instruction and to help students gain a deeper understanding of the world around them.

Science instruction will include as many hands-on activities as possible. Units will focus on the real-life application of scientific principles and will incorporate the use of science process skills. Health instruction will be considered a part of the science curriculum and will focus on learning about nutrition, exercise, and elements of healthful living.

Although students will receive Art and Music instruction outside the regular classroom, I will integrate the creative arts with core subjects whenever possible in order to enhance enjoyment of instruction and foster creative growth of all students.

My belief is that all subject areas are of great importance but that language arts are particularly crucial because they provide essential communication skills useful in all areas. For that reason, I will stress the practice of writing skills with the use of journals for all subjects.

In every subject area, the same work assignments will be given to all students, but adjustments will be made as needed in order to meet the needs of students working at varying skill levels (e.g., extra help and/or extra time to complete assignments for lower-level students; early finisher/enrichment activities for higher-level students).

Lessons will be structured to address different modalities and learning styles of students. Activities and lessons will be planned with the goal of incorporating all levels of Bloom's taxonomy in order to make sure that students develop the proper foundation for future learning, as well as the ability to apply what they have learned to real life.

Verification:
Charleston County Curriculum Guides (grade 5)
National Geography Standards
South Carolina English Language Arts Framework (grades 4–5)
South Carolina Mathematics Framework (grades 3–6)
South Carolina Visual and Performing Arts Framework (grades 3–5)
South Carolina Science Framework (grades 3–6)
Treasury of Literature—Out of This World by Harcourt Brace & Co.
Spelling and Vocabulary and *English* by Houghton Mifflin
United States and Its Neighbors by Macmillan/McGraw-Hill
Exploring Your World by Silver Burdett & Ginn
Destinations in Science by Addison-Wesley
Journeys in Science by Laidlaw Educational Publishers
Being Healthy by Harcourt Brace Jovanovich

IV. Units of Instruction

Language Arts

A. Getting Acquainted Unit
Duration: 1 week

Unit Objectives:
1. The students will use language arts skills to complete Personal Profile Sheets and Learning Style Assessment/Student Interest Surveys (attachments A, B).
2. The students will follow directions in organizing notebooks and journals to be used during the upcoming schoolyear.
3. Students and teacher will get to know each other.

The purpose for this unit is to prepare students for the upcoming schoolyear. During this time, students will get organized, turn in supplies, prepare notebooks and journals for the schoolyear, and complete surveys designed to help the teacher see the strengths and weaknesses of students. The teacher will assign cubbyholes/lockers, explain the use of journals, and go over various class-related topics (behavior expectations, daily schedule, etc.) Students and teacher will participate in various activities designed to help them get to know each another and establish positive relationships.

B. Challenges Unit
Duration: 6 weeks
Theme 1—Challenges at School
Theme 2—Challenges at Home
Theme 3—Understanding Others

Unit Objectives:
1. Students will demonstrate skills in reading, writing, and spelling through written work, projects, use of journals, and assessments (goal #3).
2. Students will evaluate and analyze the stories in this unit (goal #1) and consider the stories in comparison to their own personal experience and observation (goal #2) in order to construct meaning.

Theme 1—Weeks 1 and 2: *The Kid in the Red Jacket* by Barbara Park
    Reading: Cause and effect
    Language: Quotation marks
    Spelling: Short vowels

a. Introduce unit, theme and story; go over vocabulary; begin journal writing
b. Discuss cause and effect within story; write about cause and effect in journals
c. Discuss respect for the feelings of others
d. Write friendly letter to Howard about how to make friends
e. Stress use of quotation marks within story; continue journal writing
f. Review story and skills learned; summarize and analyze story in journals
g. Give assessment; check for mastery; revise as necessary
h. Enrichment/Early Finishers: books dealing with challenges at school; worksheets

Theme 1—Week 3: *In the Year of the Boar and Jackie Robinson* by Bette Bao Lord
    Reading: Making predictions; drawing conclusions; structural and context clues
    Language: Exclamatory sentences; personal narrative
    Spelling: Long a and long e sounds

a. Introduce story; vocabulary; long a and long e sounds; write in journals
b. Discuss use of exclamatory sentences and personal narrative; have students write their own personal narratives in journals (to be shared)
c. Discuss making predictions; drawing conclusions; structural and contextual clues; share personal narratives from journals
d. Discuss multicultural issues in story; refer to multiculturalism in journals
e. Review story and skills learned; summarize and analyze story in journals
f. Give assessment; check for mastery; revise as necessary
g. Enrichment/Early Finishers: library books dealing with challenges at school; worksheets

Theme 2—Week 4: *Whose Side Are You On?* by Emily Moore
    Reading: Elements of a story; test-taking strategies
    Language: Contractions
    Spelling: Long i and long o sounds

a. Introduce theme and story; vocabulary; use of contractions; long i and long o sounds
b. Discuss elements of a story; write about story elements in journals
c. Discuss test-taking strategies; journal response to related prompt
d. Review story and skills learned; summarize and analyze story in journals
e. Give assessment; check for mastery; revise as necessary
f. Enrichment/Early Finishers: library books dealing with challenges at home; worksheets

Theme 2—Week 5: *Pride of Puerto Rico* by Paul Robert Walker
    Reading: Reading nonfiction; review of cause and effect; review of making predictions and drawing conclusions
    Language: Ellipses
    Spelling: /oo/ and /yoo/ sounds

a. Introduce story; vocabulary; use of ellipses and words with /oo/ and /yoo/ in story
b. Discuss difference between fiction and nonfiction; write nonfiction paragraphs in journals
c. Review cause and effect; review making predictions and drawing conclusions
d. Review story and skills learned; summarize and analyze story in journals
e. Give assessment; check for mastery; revise as necessary
f. Enrichment/Early Finishers: library books dealing with challenges at home; worksheets

Theme 3—Week 6: *Sarah, Plain and Tall* by Patricia MacLachlan
    Reading: Making inferences; review of cause and effect; review of making predictions and drawing conclusions
    Language: Subjects; predicates; sentences
    Spelling: /o/ and /oo/

a. Introduce theme and story; vocabulary; use of /o/ and /oo/ words within story; subjects, predicates, and sentences
b. Introduce making inferences; review cause and effect; review making predictions and drawing conclusions; write in journals
c. Project: pictoral summary and analysis of story
d. Review story and compare to others in "Challenges" unit
e. Give assessment for story; check for mastery; revise as necessary
f. End-of-unit assessment
g. Enrichment/Early Finishers: library books dealing with understanding others; worksheets

C. Yesteryear Unit
Duration: 5 weeks
    Theme 1—Early America
    Theme 2—Women Who Led the Way
    Theme 3—Interpreting the Past

Unit Objectives:
1. Students will demonstrate skills in reading, writing, and spelling through written work, projects, use of journals, and assessment (goal #3).
2. Students will evaluate and analyze the stories in this unit (goal #1) and consider the stories in comparison to their own personal experience and observation (goal #2) in order to construct meaning.

Theme 1—Week 1: *The Sign of the Beaver* by Elizabeth George Speare
    Reading: Elements of a story; summarizing; reference sources
    Language: Sentences
    Spelling: Homophones

a. Introduce unit, theme, and story; vocabulary; sentences
b. Discuss use of homophones; elements of a story; journal writing
c. Discuss reference sources; summarize and analyze story in journals
d. Project: make story object of choice with craft sticks
e. Give assessment; check for mastery; revise as necessary
f. Enrichment/Early Finishers: library books dealing with early Americans; worksheets; puzzlers

Theme 1—Week 2: *The Riddle of Penncroft Farm* by Dorothea Jensen
    Reading: Paraphrasing; writing how-to paragraphs; graphic aids
    Language: Common and proper nouns
    Spelling: pre and pro words

a. Introduce story, vocabulary; give background about setting of American Revolution

b. Discuss common and proper nouns in story; journal writing about nouns
c. Discuss paraphrasing; paraphrase in journal
d. Write how-to paragraph and illustrate it
e. Give assessment; check for mastery; revise as necessary
f. Enrichment/Early Finishers: library books dealing with the American Revolution; worksheets

Theme 2—Weeks 3 and 4: *A Long Way to Go* by Zibby Oneal
  Reading: Author's purpose; paraphrasing; poetry
  Language: Conjunctions
  Spelling: dis and de words

a. Introduce theme and story; vocabulary; conjunctions
b. Discuss author's purpose; review paraphrasing; paraphrase in journals
c. Social studies connection: the women's suffrage movement and the Nineteenth Amendment
d. Research and do oral reports on leaders in women's suffrage movement
e. Cultural awareness: voting rights for African Americans and Native Americans
f. Conjunction activity; journal writing
g. Introduce poetry; write poem for journal using prompt
h. Review story and skills learned; summarize and analyze story in journals
i. Give assessment; check for mastery; revise as necessary
j. Enrichment/Early Finishers: library books dealing with voting rights and women's suffrage movement

Theme 3—Week 5: *The House of Dies Drear* by Virginia Hamilton
  Reading: Multiple-meaning words; library skills
  Language: Single quotation marks
  Spelling: sion and tion words

a. Introduce theme, story and vocabulary; multiple-meaning words; journal writing
b. Discuss use of single quotation marks; write with single quotation marks in journals
c. Discuss library skills; write about a special place in journals
d. Review story and skills learned; summarize and analyze in journals
e. Give assessment; check for mastery; revise as necessary
f. Enrichment/Early Finishers: library books also by Virginia Hamilton; worksheets; puzzlers

Theme 3—Week 6: *The Bells of Christmas* also by Virginia Hamilton
  Reading: Context clues; paraphrasing and summarizing; compare and contrast different works by same author
  Language: Adjectives
  Spelling: ible and able words

a. Introduce story; vocabulary; use of adjectives in story; ible and able words
b. Compare/contrast different works by same author; journal writing
c. Discuss context clues; review paraphrasing/summarizing
d. Review story and skills learned; summarize and analyze story in journals
e. Give assessment; check for mastery; revise as necessary
f. Enrichment/Early Finishers: library books also by Virginia Hamilton; worksheets; puzzles

Mathematics

A. The USA Yesterday and Today—Chapter 1: Building Number Sense: Place Value, Adding and Subtracting Unit
Duration: 3 weeks

Unit Objectives:
Students will:
1. Read, write, and round whole numbers through billions (items 1–7 meet goal #2).
2. Compare and order whole numbers.
3. Add and subtract whole numbers.
4. Relate addition and subtraction.
5. Estimate differences and sums.
6. Find facts from texts and pictures (goal #3).
7. Write about math concepts in journals (goal #1).

Week 1:
a. Lessons 1–5 in text; write in journals
b. Read aloud: *Counting on Frank* by Rod Clement
c. Daily oral math; problem of the week
d. Use manipulatives and visual aids
e. Work individually, in small groups, and in whole-group settings
f. Real-world connection project: find printed material that reflects topics covered in unit (place value as shown in U.S. budget figures, distances on U.S. maps, etc.)
g. Review for quiz with game or activity
h. Give quiz; check for mastery; revise as necessary
i. Enrichment/Early Finishers: place value worksheets; puzzlers; mind bogglers

Week 2:
a. Lessons 6–10 in text; write in journals
b. Daily oral math; problem of the week
c. Use manipulatives and visual aids
d. Work individually, in small groups, and in whole-group settings
e. Real-world connection project: writing activity involving collection of data at home (estimate cost for what a family of four will eat for one day)
f. Give quiz; check for mastery; revise if necessary
g. Enrichment/Early Finishers: estimation worksheets; puzzlers; mind bogglers

Week 3:
a. Lessons 11–16 in text; write in journals
b. Daily oral math; problem of the week
c. Use manipulatives and visual aids
d. Work individually, in small groups, and in whole-group settings
e. Real-world connection project: use an atlas to chart the distance traveled on an imaginary family vacation
f. Listen to "The Flight of the Bumblebee"; notice mathematical rhythm patterns
g. Review lessons 1–16; give chapter test; check for mastery; revise as necessary
h. Enrichment/Early Finishers: chart worksheets; puzzlers; mind bogglers

B. People at Work—Chapter 2: Multiplying Whole Numbers Unit
Duration: 2 weeks

Unit Objectives:
Students will:
1. Use multiplication properties and patterns (items 1–7 meet goal #2).
2. Estimate products.
3. Multiply by one-digit factors.
4. Find multiples and least-common multiples.

5. Problem-solve; determine if too much or too little information (goal #3).
6. Multiply money; multiply by two- and three-digit factors.
7. Write about math concepts in journals (goal #1).

   Week 1:
a. Lessons 1–6 in text; write in journals
b. Daily oral math; problem of the week
c. Use manipulatives and visual aids
d. Work individually, in small groups, and in whole-group settings
e. Real-world connection project: use multiplication to figure cost for monthly office supplies
f. Review for quiz with mental math activity
g. Give quiz; check for mastery; revise as necessary
h. Enrichment/Early Finishers: multiplication worksheets; puzzlers; mind bogglers

   Week 2:
a. Lessons 7–12 in text; write in journals
b. Daily oral math; problem of the week
c. Use manipulatives and visual aids
d. Work individually, in small groups, and in whole-group settings
e. Real-world connection project: use multiplication of money to figure salaries for various occupations based on hourly wages
f. Review lessons 1–12; give chapter test; check for mastery; revise as necessary
g. Enrichment/Early Finishers: multiplication worksheets; puzzlers; mind bogglers

C. Collections—Chapter 3: Understanding Division Unit
Duration: 3 weeks

   Unit Objectives:
   Students will:
1. Relate multiplication and division as inverse operations (items 1–7 meet goal #2).
2. Estimate quotients.
3. Divide two-, three-, and four-digit numbers.
4. Make and use tables to solve problems and interpret data.
5. Estimate and find averages.
6. Divide money (goal #3).
7. Write about math concepts in journals (goal #1).

   Week 1:
a. Lessons 1–5 in text; write in journals
b. Daily oral math; problem of the week
c. Use manipulatives and visual aids
d. Work individually, in small groups, and in whole-group settings
e. Real-world connection project: use division to reduce recipe ingredients
f. Play review game involving division
g. Give quiz; check for mastery; revise as necessary
h. Enrichment/Early Finishers: division worksheets; puzzlers; mind bogglers

   Week 2:
a. Lessons 6–10 in text; write in journals
b. Daily oral math; problem of the week
c. Use manipulatives and visual aids
d. Work individually, in small groups, and in whole-group settings
e. Real-world connection project: use tables to figure monthly payments based on interest rates

f. Review lessons 6–10; give quiz; check for mastery; revise as necessary
g. Enrichment/Early Finishers: table worksheets; puzzlers; mind bogglers

Week 3:
a. Lessons 11–15 in text; write in journals
b. Daily oral math; problem of the week
c. Use manipulatives and visual aids
d. Work individually, in small groups, and in whole-group settings
e. Real-world connection project: use division of money to figure discounts on sale items
f. Review lessons 1–15; give chapter test; check for mastery; revise as necessary
g. Enrichment/Early Finishers: dividing money worksheets, mind bogglers

D. Sports—Chapter 4: Dividing by Two-Digit Divisors Unit
Duration: 2 weeks

Unit Objectives:
Students will:
1. Divide by tens with and without a remainder (items 1–10 meet goal #2).
2. Estimate quotients.
3. Use compatible numbers.
4. Divide two- and three-digit dividends by multiples of ten.
5. Divide two- and three-digit dividends by two-digit divisors.
6. Change an estimated quotient that is too low or too high.
7. Use experimentation to solve nonroutine problems (goal #3).
8. Find factors, common factors, and greatest common factor.
9. Tell if a number is prime or composite.
10. Write about concepts in journals (goal #1).

Week 1:
a. Lessons 1–7 in text; write in journals
b. Daily oral math; problem of the week
c. Use manipulatives and visual aids
d. Work individually, in small groups, and in whole-group settings
e. Real-world connection project: use division to figure which of two pro baseball players had the better base-stealing record
f. Review lessons 1–7
g. Give quiz; check for mastery; revise as necessary
h. Enrichment/Early Finishers: division worksheets; puzzlers; mind bogglers

Week 2:
a. Lessons 8–14 in text; write in journals
b. Daily oral math; problem of the week
c. Use manipulatives and visual aids
d. Work individually, in small groups, and in whole-group settings
e. Real-world career connection project: do exercise showing how an architect could rearrange the windows in a building design to meet set criteria
f. Review lessons 1–14; play review game
g. Give chapter test; check for mastery; revise as necessary
h. Enrichment/Early Finishers: worksheets; puzzlers; brain teasers

E. What's Your Choice?—Chapter 5: Applying Knowledge of Time, Data, and Graphs in Making Choices Unit
Duration: 2 weeks

Unit Objectives:
Students will:
1. Tell time; use units of time; estimate units of time (all items meet goal #2).
2. Find elapsed time; add and subtract units of time.
3. Read and interpret bar graphs, pictographs, line graphs, and circle graphs.
4. Collect and organize data.
5. Make various types of graphs.
6. Use guess-and-test strategy to solve nonroutine problems (goal #1).
7. Describe data using mean, median, mode, and range.
8. Use calculators to solve problems (goal #3).
9. Write about math concepts in journals (goal #1).

Week 1:
a. Lessons 1–7 in text; write in journals
b. Daily oral math; problem of the week
c. Use manipulatives and visual aids
d. Work individually, in small groups, and in whole-group settings
e. Play "Beat the Clock" game
f. Review lessons 1–7
g. Give quiz; check for mastery; revise as necessary
h. Enrichment/Early Finishers: time and graphing worksheets; brain teasers

Week 2:
a. Lessons 8–12 in text; write in journals
b. Daily oral math; problem of the week
c. Work individually, in small groups, and in whole-group settings
d. Use manipulatives and visual aids
e. Real-world connection project: determine amount of money taken in by school cafeteria over various periods; graph results
f. Review lessons 1–12
g. Give chapter test; check for mastery; revise as necessary
h. Enrichment/Early Finishers: money worksheets; puzzlers; mind bogglers

Science

A. Ecosystems Unit
Duration: 6 weeks
 Theme 1—Getting Food
 Theme 2—Food Webs
 Theme 3—The Environment

Unit Objectives:
1. Students will make observations, collect and analyze data, and draw conclusions using the science process skills (goal #1).
2. Students will talk, write, and communicate about science concepts through the use of journals (goal #3).

Theme 1—Week 1:
a. Introduce unit and vocabulary

b. Explain, do, and discuss experiment in creating an ecosystem
c. Observe experiment results throughout week; record data and draw conclusions
d. Write in journals
e. Read "How Living Things Get Energy" (lesson 1)
f. Enrichment/Early Finishers: research an ecosystem; worksheets

Theme 1—Week 2:
a. Read "Classifying Consumers" (lesson 2); add to vocabulary
b. Make a fungus garden in small groups
c. Observe garden for several days; record data and draw conclusions; write in journals
d. Science & literature connection: read *All Things Are Linked* (excerpt from *The Crest and the Hide* by Harold Courlander)
e. Give Chapter 1 quiz; check for mastery; revise as needed
f. Enrichment/Early Finishers: read book *The Crest and the Hide*

Theme 2—Weeks 3 and 4:
a. Read and discuss "Interactions of Living Things" (lesson 1)
b. Discuss the food chain; go over vocabulary
c. Do food chain activity; describe in journals
d. Discuss the food web; perform "Oh Deer" whole-group activity (Project WILD)
e. Write in journals
f. Science & math connection: make graphs of population data and make predictions about increases/decreases
g. Review Chapter 2
h. Give Chapter 2 quiz; check for mastery; revise as needed
i. Enrichment/Early Finishers: research deer population growth

Theme 3—Weeks 5 and 6:
a. Introduce "The Environment" by reading "Habitats and Ecosystems" (lesson 1)
b. Do experiment, "How Do Individuals Compete?" using seeds, potting soil, and two shallow pans
c. Monitor results of experiment; record, collect, and analyze data; write in journals
d. Read "Changes in Ecosystems" (lesson 2)
e. Discuss vocabulary; describe how materials are recycled in ecosystems
f. Guest speaker: forestry technician discusses ecosystems and jobs in forestry
g. Review Ecosystems unit
h. Assessment on Chapters 1–3
i. Enrichment/Early Finishers: research an animal habitat; worksheets

B. The Earth's Resources Unit
Duration: 6 weeks
Theme 1—Renewable Resources
Theme 2—Nonrenewable Resources
Theme 3—The Rock Cycle

Unit Objectives:
1. Students will make observations, collect and analyze data, and draw conclusions using the science process skills (goal #1).
2. Students will talk, write, and communicate about science concepts through the use of journals. (goal #3)
3. Students will relate instructional experiences to everyday life (goal #2).

Theme 1—Week 1:
a. Introduce unit and vocabulary
b. Read and discuss "The Earth's Resources" (Chapter 4)
c. Experiment: getting fresh water from salt water
d. Record, analyze, and collect data; write in journals
e. Science & math connection: calculate how much water a family uses in a week taking showers versus baths
f. Social Studies connection: compare precipitation rates in United States and world

Theme 1—Week 2:
a. Read and discuss "Air: A Vital Resource"
b. Small-group activity: research and make class presentations about causes and sources of pollution
c. Record data in journals
d. Discuss acid rain in the environment
e. Review Chapter 4
f. Give Chapter 4 quiz; check for mastery; revise as needed
g. Enrichment/Early Finishers: research pollution; worksheets

Theme 2—Week 3:
a. Read and discuss "Nonrenewable Resources" (Chapter 5)
b. Activity "Renewable or Nonrenewable Resource?" (from DHEC Workshop book)
c. Show SCE&G video, "An Astounding Adventure"
d. Write in journals
e. Social Studies connection: compare fossil fuel deposits in United States and world
f. Enrichment/Early Finishers: research fossil-fuel shortage; worksheets

Theme 2—Week 4:
a. Read about ways to conserve and recycle natural resources
b. Small-group science projects: research ways to conserve/recycle resources; share results with class
c. Collect information and write in journals
d. Review Chapter 5
e. Give Chapter 5 quiz; check for mastery; revise as necessary

Theme 3—Week 5:
a. Introduce the rock cycle with lesson on Montserrat
b. Go over vocabulary
c. Write in journals
d. Overview with lesson about the rock cycle
e. Read and discuss *The Magic School Bus—Inside the Earth*
f. Small-group activity: grow your own rock gardens
g. Guest speaker: geologist
h. Enrichment/Early Finishers: worksheets; rock books in class library

Theme 3—Week 6:
a. Lessons and activities on three rock types (sedimentary, metamorphic, igneous)
b. Write in journals
c. Continue rock gardens
d. Lesson on uses of rocks
e. Rock-n-Roll Review game
f. Give rock cycle quiz
g. Give unit assessment; check for mastery; revise as necessary
h. Enrichment/Early Finishers: rock books in class library; worksheets

Social Studies

A. Geography of the United States Unit
Duration: 6 weeks

Unit Objectives:
1. Students will learn the five fundamental themes of geography (goal #3).
2. Students will use and review map and globe skills (goal #1).
3. Students will learn about the five regions of the United States (goal #4).
4. Students will write about concepts in journals.
5. Students will read about and discuss current events (goal #2).

Week 1:
a. Introduce the five fundamental themes of geography; write in journals
b. Writing task: why learning about geography is important
c. Lesson reviewing use of map and globe skills
d. Define key vocabulary
e. Play "Where in the World Am I?" using the atlas
f. Share and discuss current events articles (general geography)
g. Enrichment/Early Finishers: geography skills worksheets; puzzlers

Week 2:
a. Introduce "The American Land" (Chapter 1)
b. Define key vocabulary; write in journals
c. Discuss climate and natural resources of the United States
d. Read and discuss "Our Country's National Parks"
e. Share and discuss current events articles (natural resources)
f. Summarize and review Chapter 1
g. Chapter 1 quiz; check for mastery; revise as necessary
h. Enrichment/Early Finishers: chapter worksheets; puzzlers

Week 3:
a. Read and discuss "Our Country's Regions"
b. Define key vocabulary; write in journals
c. Lesson on the Northeast region
d. Read Robert Frost poem, "New Hampshire" (celebration of rural New England life)
e. Share and discuss current events articles (New England)
f. Quiz on the Northeast region; check for mastery; revise as necessary
g. Enrichment/Early Finishers: chapter worksheets; puzzlers; books about United States geography

Week 4:
a. Lesson on the Southeast region; write in journals
b. Compare/contrast Northeast and Southeast regions
c. Write a letter to the textbook editor about "your" Southeast region
d. Share and discuss current events articles (Southeast)
e. Small-group activity: oral presentations about tourism in the South using South Carolina Travel Guides as reference tools
f. Quiz on Southeast region; check for mastery; revise as necessary
g. Enrichment/Early Finishers: chapter worksheets; puzzlers

Week 5:
a. Lesson on the Middle West region; write in journals
b. Discuss agriculture in the Middle West and the importance of the Great Lakes

c. Lesson on the Southwest region
d. Discuss natural resources found in the Southwest region
e. Compare/contrast resources of the Southwest (oil industry) with those of the Middle West (agriculture and industry)
f. Share and discuss current events (Middle West or Southwest)
g. Quiz on Middle West and Southwest regions; check for mastery; revise as necessary
h. Enrichment/Early Finishers: chapter worksheets; additional research topics

Week 6:
a. Lesson on the West region; write in journals
b. Writing activity: suggest ways to help with water-supply problems in the West
c. Compare/contrast each of the five U.S. regions
d. Share and discuss current events (U.S. regional differences)
e. Review for unit test
f. Give unit test
g. Enrichment/Early Finishers: chapter worksheets; books about regions of the United States

B. Settling the Americas Unit
Duration: 3 weeks

Unit Objectives:
1. Students will learn about the civilizations of the first Americans (goal #4).
2. Students will learn how the different environments of North America influenced Indian culture (goal #3).
3. Students will write about concepts in journals.
4. Students will read about and discuss current events (goal #2).

Week 1:
a. Introduce unit and key vocabulary; write in journals
b. Read and discuss "The First Americans" (Chapter 3)
c. Locate and describe the route taken by the first Americans
d. Lesson on farming techniques of the first Americans
e. Discuss similarities and differences between Incan, Mayan, and Aztec civilizations
f. Share and discuss current events articles (farming)
g. Enrichment/Early Finishers: chapter worksheets; books about ancient Indians

Week 2:
a. Read and discuss "Early North American Cultures"; write in journals
b. Compare/contrast the cultures of the Anasazi and the Woodland people
c. Read and discuss "Learning about the Past"
d. Activity: have each student make and illustrate a timeline of his or her life
e. Share and discuss current events articles (multiculturalism)
f. Quiz on Chapter 3; check for mastery; revise as necessary
g. Enrichment/Early Finishers: chapter worksheets; research a Native American tribe

Week 3:
a. Read and discuss "The Indians of North America" (Chapter 4); write in journals
b. Discuss how different cultures developed in response to different environmental conditions
c. Group activity: have students analyze points of view of the Indians and the Europeans in the exercise, "Who Has the Right to the Land?"
d. Small-group activity: dramatic oral presentations from four small groups assuming the roles of the Southwest Indians, the Eastern Woodlands Indians, the Plains Indians, and the Hunters and Gatherers of the West

e. Share and discuss current events articles (land rights)
f. Review unit; give unit test
g. Enrichment/Early Finishers: chapter worksheets; books about land disputes

C. Europeans Come to the Americas Unit
Duration: 3 weeks

Unit Objectives:
1. Students will learn about the motivations and accomplishments of the explorers who came to North America (items 1 and 2 meet goal #4).
2. Students will recognize the impact of explorations in shaping American history.
3. Students will write about concepts in journals.

Week 1:
a. Introduce unit and key vocabulary; write in journals
b. Read and discuss "Europeans Reach America" (Chapter 5)
c. Small-group project: students will be divided into small groups, and each group will make a presentation about the motivation and accomplishments of one of the explorers
d. Share and discuss current events articles (current explorations)
e. Review Chapter 5
f. Quiz on Chapter 5; check for mastery; revise as necessary
g. Enrichment/Early Finishers: chapter worksheets; books about explorers

Week 2:
a. Read and discuss "The Search for the Northwest Passage" and "England and Spain Compete" (Chapter 6); write in journals
b. Map skills practice: have students color-code a map of America to show areas claimed by the French, English, Spanish, and Dutch
c. Group activity: divide class in half and let them act out the competition between England and Spain over land in North America
d. Writing task: "Was Sir Francis Drake a hero or a thief? Explain your answer."
e. Share and discuss current events articles (piracy)
f. Enrichment/Early Finishers: chapter worksheets; puzzlers

Week 3:
a. Read and discuss "England's First Settlement" and "The French Begin New France" (Chapter 6); write in journals
b. Compare/contrast North American settlements of the French and English
c. Multicultural perspective and map skills practice: how can the influence of the French and English be seen on a map of North America today?
d. Share and discuss current events articles (multiculturalism)
e. Review Unit 3
f. Give end-of-unit test
g. Enrichment/Early Finishers: chapter and unit worksheets; classroom library

Health

A. Your Feelings and Actions Unit
Duration: 3 weeks

Unit Objectives:
1. Students will be able to identify their own needs (goal #1).
2. Students will learn how our needs affect our feelings and actions (goal #1).
3. Students will learn how to choose healthful ways to handle their feelings (goal #3).

4. Students will write concepts in journals.

   Week 1:
   a. Read and discuss "Identifying Your Needs"
   b. Define key vocabulary; write in journals
   c. Create and illustrate your own "personal needs pyramid"
   d. Enrichment/Early Finishers: select book from classroom library

   Week 2:
   a. Read and discuss "Your Needs Affect Your Feelings & Actions"
   b. Define key vocabulary; write in journals
   c. Have students "act out" words that express various feelings (angry, sad, happy, confused, etc.)
   d. Enrichment/Early Finishers: select book from classroom library

   Week 3:
   a. Read and discuss "Choosing Healthful Ways to Handle Your Feelings"
   b. Define vocabulary; write in journals
   c. Pose hypothetical problem situations and have students suggest ways to handle them
   d. Review unit
   e. Give unit test; check for mastery; revise as necessary
   f. Enrichment/Early Finishers: select book from classroom library

B. Taking Care of Your Health Unit
Duration: 4 weeks

   Unit Objectives:
   1. Students will identify dependable sources of health information (goal #2).
   2. Students will learn about how to properly care for teeth, eyes, and ears (goal #3).
   3. Students will write concepts in journals.

   Week 1:
   a. Read and discuss "Getting Ready to Care for Your Health"
   b. Define vocabulary; write in journals
   c. Compare dependable sources of health information to unreliable sources or myths
   d. Enrichment/Early Finishers: select book from classroom library

   Week 2:
   a. Read and discuss "Taking Care of Your Teeth & Gums"
   b. Define vocabulary; write in journals
   c. Do "tooth decay experiment" using eggshells, vinegar, soda, and water
   d. Enrichment/Early Finishers: select book from classroom library

   Week 3:
   a. Read and Discuss "Taking Care of Your Eyes & Vision"
   b. Define vocabulary; write in journals
   c. Writing task: "What if you lost your eyesight?"
   d. Enrichment/Early Finishers: select book from classroom library

   Week 4:
   a. Read and discuss "Taking Care of Your Ears & Hearing"
   b. Define vocabulary; write in journals
   c. Guest speaker: health care professional
   d. Review unit
   e. Give unit test; check for mastery; revise as necessary

f. Enrichment/Early Finishers: select book from classroom library

C. Food and Activity for a Healthy Body Unit
Duration: 5 weeks

Unit Objectives:
1. Students will learn why the human body needs food (goal #3).
2. Students will learn the components of a balanced diet (goal #3).
3. Students will identify ways that exercise improves health (goal #3).
4. Students will learn daily practices for fitness (goal #2).
5. Students will learn how to balance activity and rest (goal #3).
6. Students will write about concepts in journals.

Week 1:
a. Read and discuss "Your Body Needs Food"
b. Define vocabulary; write in journals
c. Small-group activity: have students do oral presentations on nutrients (one per group)
d. Enrichment/Early Finishers: research a particular nutrient

Week 2:
a. Read and discuss "Which Nutrients Help You Use Other Nutrients?"
b. Define vocabulary; write in journals
c. Group activity: make and illustrate chart showing sources and uses of vitamins
d. Enrichment/Early Finishers: research a particular vitamin

Week 3:
a. Read and discuss "Variety and Balance in What You Eat"
b. Define vocabulary; write in journals
c. Real-world connection: make grocery list for your family based on the Food Wheel
d. Enrichment/Early Finishers: compare fast-food menus for proper diet

Week 4:
a. Read and discuss "Exercise and Your Health"
b. Define vocabulary; write in journals
c. Small-group activity: have students in three groups create murals showing people engaged in activities improving endurance, strengthening muscles, and increasing flexibility
d. Enrichment/Early Finishers: research benefits of a particular exercise or activity

Week 5:
a. Read and discuss "Daily Practices for Fitness" and "Balancing Activity with Rest and Sleep"
b. Define vocabulary; write in journals
c. Have students create daily activity schedules, including periods for exercise and rest
d. Review unit
e. Give unit test; check for mastery; revise as necessary
f. Enrichment/Early Finishers: choose a book on fitness from classroom library

Creative Arts
Students will receive instruction for art and music outside the regular classroom. However, every effort will be made to include creative arts activities with the regular curriculum as follows:

Language Arts: During the "Getting Acquainted" unit, the "various activities designed to help" students and teacher "get to know one another" will include at least one creative art activity. During the "Challenges" unit, students will create pictoral summaries of *Sarah, Plain and Tall*. During the "Yesteryear" unit, students will create objects of choice from the story *The Sign of the Beaver.* Students will illustrate a how-to paragraph while studying *The Riddle of Penncroft Farm.*

Mathematics: Students will listen to "The Flight of the Bumblebee" during the "USA Yesterday and Today" unit in order to note mathematical rhythm patterns.

Science: During the study of the rock cycle, students will create rock gardens. Journals will include illustrations of various scientific concepts.

Social Studies: During the "Settling the Americas" unit, students will make and illustrate time-lines of their own lives. During the same unit, students will assume the roles of Native Americans representing several different groups. During the unit entitled "Europeans Come to the Americas," students will act out the competition between the English and Spanish over North American lands.

Health: During the "Your Feelings and Actions" unit, students will create and illustrate their own "personal needs pyramids." Later in the unit, they will "act out" words that express various feelings. In the "Food and Activity for a Healthy Body" unit, students will make and illustrate charts showing sources and uses of vitamins. Near the end of the same unit, students will create murals showing people engaged in various healthful activities.

V. Instructional Materials and Resources

Language Arts

A. Getting Acquainted Unit
1. 24 copies of each of the surveys (see attached)
2. Supply list check-off sheet
3. Library books for Early Finishers

B. Challenges Unit
1. *Out of this World* textbooks (classroom set)
2. Library books that deal with challenges
3. Overhead and screen
4. Transparency with vocabulary
5. 24 copies of various worksheets
6. Models of writing forms (expository paragraph, personal narrative, etc.)
7. Various posters and charts pertaining to unit
8. Early Finishers' worksheets, puzzles, challenge cards, etc.

C. Yesteryear Unit
1. *Out of this World* textbooks (classroom set)
2. Library books that deal with the past
3. Overhead and screen
4. Transparencies of vocabulary
5. 24 copies of various worksheets
6. Models of writing forms (expository paragraph, personal narrative, etc.)
7. Variety of charts and posters
8. Early Finishers' worksheets, puzzles, challenge cards, etc.

Mathematics

A. The USA Yesterday and Today—Chapter 1: Building Number Sense: Place Value, Adding and Subtracting Unit
1. *Exploring Your World* textbooks (classroom set)
2. *Counting on Frank* by Rod Clement
3. Various newspapers and magazines
4. Manipulatives: base-ten blocks, number cubes, counters, bill sets, dice
5. Charts, index cards, and number lines
6. "The Flight of the Bumblebee" on cassette tape and tape player
7. Multiplication games: Bingo, Quizmo, etc.
8. World map/atlas
9. Overhead and screen
10. Early Finishers' worksheets, puzzles, challenge cards, brain teasers, etc.

B. People at Work—Chapter 2: Multiplying Whole Numbers Unit
1. *Exploring Your World* textbooks (classroom set)
2. 1–100 number tables
3. Posters and charts
4. Manipulatives: base-ten blocks, number cubes, counters, bill sets, dice
5. Charts, index cards, and number lines
6. World map/atlas
7. Multiplication games: Bingo, Quizmo, etc.
8. Calculators
9. Overhead and screen
10. Early Finishers' worksheets, puzzles, challenge sheets, brain teasers, etc.

C. Collections—Chapter 3: Understanding Division Unit
1. *Exploring Your World* textbooks (classroom set)
2. Problem-solving cards
3. Division games and multiplication games: Bingo, Quizmo, etc.
4. Manipulatives: base-ten blocks, number cubes, counters, bill sets, dice
5. Charts, index cards, and number lines
6. World map/atlas
7. Recipes
8. Overhead and screen
9. Early Finishers' worksheets, puzzles, challenge sheets, brain teasers, etc.

D. Sports—Chapter 4: Dividing by Two-Digit Divisors Unit
1. *Exploring Your World* textbooks (classroom set)
2. Manipulatives: base-ten blocks, number cubes, counters, bill sets, dice
3. Charts, index cards, and number lines
4. Division game
5. Posters and charts
6. Pro baseball cards; base-stealing stats
7. Overhead and screen
8. Early Finishers' worksheets, puzzles, challenge sheets, brain teasers, etc.

E. What's Your Choice?—Chapter 5: Applying Knowledge of Time, Data, and Graphs in Making Choices Unit
1. *Exploring Your World* textbooks (classroom set)
2. Manipulatives: base-ten blocks, number cubes, counters, bill sets, dice

3. Clocks and clock models
4. Various bar, line, circle, and picto graphs
5. Charts, index cards, and number lines
6. Posters and transparencies
7. Magazines showing graphic displays of data
8. "Beat the Clock" game and calculators
9. Overhead and screen
10. Early Finishers' worksheets, puzzles, challenge sheets, brain teasers, etc.

Science

A. Ecosystems Unit
1. *Destinations in Science* textbooks (classroom set)
2. Supplies for making ecosystems: six 2-liter plastic bottles, potting soil, six plants, small animals, spray bottles, aluminum foil
3. Supplies for making fungus gardens: six damp paper towels, six jars with lids, dead leaves, twigs or food
4. Peanuts for food-chain activity
5. Supplies for "How Do Individuals Compete?" activity: paper towels, 50 carrot or beet seeds, water, potting soil, two shallow pans
6. Guest speaker: forestry technician
7. Overhead, screen, and various transparencies
8. Science process skills poster
9. Early Finishers' worksheets, puzzles, library and classroom books

B. The Earth's Resources Unit
1. *Journeys in Science* textbooks (classroom set)
2. Overhead, screen, and various transparencies
3. Science process skills poster
4. Saltwater/freshwater experiment supplies: balance with gram weights, salt, water, drinking glass, spoon, plastic wrap, rubber bands, black pepper
5. SCE&G video, "An Astounding Adventure"
6. Various rock samples
7. *National Geographic* magazine article on Montserrat
8. *The Magic School Bus—Inside the Earth* by Joanna Cole
9. Rock garden supplies: ammonia, salt, rocks, shallow dish, liquid bluing, water, food coloring
10. Guest speaker: geologist
11. Metamorphic rock activity: marshmallows, wax paper
12. Sedimentary rock activity: bread, peanut butter, celery leaves, candy bars with nuts, cream cheese
13. Igneous rock activity: matches, crayons, candles, paper plates
14. Various household items for "Uses of Rocks" lesson
15. Early Finishers' worksheets, rock puzzlers, word finds, classroom library books

Social Studies

A. Geography of the United States Unit
1. *The US and Its Neighbors* textbooks (classroom set)
2. Maps and globes of United States and the world
3. Overhead and screen
4. Various transparencies
5. Posters

6. Robert Frost poem, "New Hampshire"
7. Travel guides from the South Carolina Department of Tourism
8. Early Finishers' worksheets, puzzles, geography crosswords, classroom books

B. Settling the Americas Unit
1. *The US and Its Neighbors* textbooks (classroom set)
2. Maps and globes of the United States and world
3. Overhead and screen
4. Various transparencies
5. Posters
6. Rolls of paper for timelines
7. Early Finishers' worksheets, puzzlers, crosswords, classroom library books

C. Europeans Come to the Americas Unit
1. *The US and Its Neighbors* textbooks (classroom set)
2. Maps and globes of the United States and world
3. Overhead and screen
4. Various transparencies
5. Posters
6. 24 outline maps of America

Health

A. Your Feelings and Actions Unit
1. *Being Healthy* textbooks (classroom set)
2. Overhead and screen
3. Various transparencies
4. Posters
5. Early Finishers' health worksheets, puzzles, resource books

B. Taking Care of Your Health Unit
1. *Being Healthy* textbooks (classroom set)
2. Overhead and screen
3. Various transparencies
4. Posters
5. Magazines, journals (reliable and unreliable sources of health information)
6. Supplies for tooth decay experiment: egg shells, vinegar, soda, water, cups
7. Guest speaker: health care professional
8. Early Finishers' health worksheets, puzzles, resource books

C. Food and Activity for a Healthy Body Unit
1. *Being Healthy* textbooks (classroom set)
2. Overhead and screen
3. Various transparencies
4. Posters
5. Rolled paper for murals, paint
6. Early Finishers' health worksheets, puzzles, resource books

Creative Arts
(materials included in the above subject-area lists)

Other Resources:
Karges-Bone, L. (1995) *Authentic Instruction and Assessment.* Morristown, New Jersey: Good Apple.

VI. Assessment

Language Arts

A. Getting Acquainted Unit
1. Teacher observation

B. Challenges Unit
1. Teacher observation
2. Quizzes
3. Journal review (checklist)
4. Theme assessments (authentic and traditional)
5. End-of-unit assessment (traditional)

C. Yesteryear Unit
1. Teacher observation
2. Quizzes
3. Journal review (checklist)
4. Theme assessments (authentic and traditional)
5. End-of-unit assessment (traditional)

Mathematics

A. The USA Yesterday and Today—Chapter 1: Building Number Sense: Place Value, Adding and Subtracting Unit
1. Teacher observation
2. Problems of the week
3. Quizzes
4. Journal review (checklist)
5. Worksheets
6. Assignments
7. Projects (authentic)
8. End-of-chapter test (traditional)

B. People at Work—Chapter 2: Multiplying Whole Numbers Unit
1. Teacher observation
2. Problems of the week
3. Quizzes
4. Journal review (checklist)
5. Worksheets
6. Assignments
7. Projects (authentic)
8. End-of-chapter test (traditional)

C. Collections—Chapter 3: Understanding Division Unit
1. Teacher observation
2. Problems of the week
3. Quizzes
4. Journal review (checklist)
5. Worksheets
6. Assignments
7. Projects (authentic)
8. End-of-chapter test (traditional)

D. Sports—Chapter 4: Dividing by Two-Digit Divisors Unit
1. Teacher observation
2. Problems of the week
3. Quizzes
4. Journal review (checklist)
5. Worksheets
6. Assignments
7. Projects (authentic)
8. End-of-chapter test (traditional)

E. What's Your Choice?—Chapter 5: Applying Knowledge of Time, Data, and Graphs in Making Choices Unit
1. Teacher observation
2. Problems of the week
3. Quizzes
4. Journal review (checklist)
5. Worksheets
6. Assignments
7. Projects (authentic)
8. End-of-chapter test (traditional)

Science

A. Ecosystems Unit
1. Teacher observation
2. Journal review (checklist)
3. Chapter quizzes
4. Worksheets
5. Assignments
6. Projects (authentic)
7. End-of-unit test (traditional and authentic)

B. The Earth's Resources Unit
1. Teacher observation
2. Journal review (checklist)
3. Chapter quizzes
4. Worksheets
5. Assignments
6. Projects (authentic)
7. End-of-unit test (traditional and authentic)

Social Studies

A. Geography of the United States Unit
1. Teacher observation
2. Quizzes
3. Journal review (checklist)
4. Worksheets
5. Assignments
6. Projects (authentic)
7. End-of-unit test (traditional)

B. Settling the Americas Unit
1. Teacher observation
2. Quizzes
3. Journal review (checklist)
4. Worksheets
5. Assignments
6. Projects (authentic)
7. End-of-unit test (traditional)

C. Europeans Come to the Americas Unit
1. Teacher observation
2. Quizzes
3. Journal review (checklist)
4. Worksheets
5. Assignments
6. Projects (authentic)
7. End-of-unit test (traditional)

Health

A. Your Feelings and Actions Unit
1. Teacher observation
2. Journal review (checklist)
3. Worksheets
4. Assignments
5. Projects (authentic)
6. Unit test (traditional and authentic)

B. Taking Care of Your Health Unit
1. Teacher observation
2. Journal review (checklist)
3. Worksheets
4. Assignments
5. Projects (authentic)
6. Unit test (traditional and authentic)

C. Food and Activity for a Healthy Body Unit
1. Teacher observation
2. Journal review (checklist)
3. Worksheets
4. Assignments
5. Projects (authentic)
6. Unit test (traditional and authentic)

Creative Arts
(assessments included as part of regular subject area units)

VII. Student Records _____

1. **Grade Book**—Grades given for various assignments and assessments will be recorded in a grade book; they will be labeled by type and dated. Grades will also be entered into a computerized record-keeping program.

2. **Teacher's Student Files**—The teacher will maintain a file for each student. Included in each file will be copies of tests, work samples, test scores, progress reports (attachments C, D, and F), homework reports, parent conference forms, documentation of phone calls, and any other records pertaining to the student's performance in the classroom.

3. **Student Work Folders**—On Monday of each week, each student will take home a folder containing samples of graded materials completed during the previous week. Unless otherwise indicated, the papers will be kept at home. Also included in the folder will be a weekly progress report (attachment C). The progress report should be signed by the parent and returned along with the folder the following day.

VIII. Discipline Policy

Students are expected to comply with all rules as presented in the school's student handbook. Rules and consequences will be clearly posted in the classroom. During the first week of school, students and parents will sign Classroom Expectations contracts outlining expectations for the schoolyear. Time is set aside during the first week of school to discuss these expectations and model appropriate behavior.

IX. Procedures for Noninstructional Activities

Morning Routine—Students are given an opportunity to prepare themselves for the day. They are to come in quietly, unpack, sharpen pencils, and begin morning work.

Restroom Breaks—With the exception of emergencies, students will be given restroom breaks after Special Area (morning) and lunch (midday).

Movement between Areas—The teacher will escort students to and from Special Area, lunch, and recess. These will be considered "no talking" times. Students may read a book of choice while waiting in line.

Emergency Drills—During earthquake, fire, and tornado drills, students will be expected to line up quickly and quietly. No talking will be allowed during drills. The first student in line will open the door and lead the class out of the building following the prescribed route. This route will be posted in the room and discussed during the first week of school. Upon reaching the designated area, the teacher will check attendance.

School Assemblies—Students will be expected to be respectful and attentive during all assemblies. Misbehavior during assemblies will result in loss of privileges and/or punishment, depending on the severity of the misbehavior. Rewards will be given to students demonstrating appropriate behavior.

Field Trips—Students will be expected to behave on all field trips. Permission slips must be signed by parents before students may participate on field trips. Students who misbehave during field trips will be disciplined, based on the severity of the misbehavior. Rewards will be given for students demonstrating appropriate behavior.

X. Parent Communication

Prior to the start of the schoolyear, parents, teachers, and students will have the opportunity to discuss various expectations for the upcoming schoolyear on "Meet the Teacher Night." At that time, parents will be given supply lists, handouts, student handbooks, and various other items. Included in the packet will be an introductory letter, list of expectations, and explanation of procedures for the classroom. Those unable to attend "Meet the Teacher Night" will receive the packet during the first week of school.

Every Monday, each student will take home a student work folder. The folder will contain samples of schoolwork from the previous week, as well as a weekly progress report (attachment C). This report will indicate any behavior problems and/or missing assignments. If a student's behavior is deemed by the teacher to be unacceptable for the week, a daily behavior sheet (attachment D) will also be completed the following week. Unless otherwise indicated, parents will keep papers included in the folder and sign the folder and the weekly progress report(s). Students will be responsible for returning these items the following day. Also sent home on Mondays will be the school newsletter, any other school-to-parent communication, and a weekly classroom newsletter (attachment E). The classroom newsletter will let parents know our short-range plans for the upcoming week and any other pertinent classroom information.

Parent-teacher conferences will be scheduled at least twice yearly, and more often if it is deemed necessary. Interim progress reports (attachment F) will be sent home to parents during the middle of each nine-week period. Report cards will be sent home every nine weeks.

All parent-teacher communications will be documented in the teacher's student files. Parents will be sent notes about good behavior as well as about any unacceptable behavior that may occur. Likewise, I will place phone calls to parents on a regular basis, during which time I will provide both positive and negative feedback, as appropriate. A phone log will be maintained to document these calls.

I believe very strongly that the relationship between parent(s) and teacher is crucial to the personal and academic growth of every child. For this reason, I will make every effort to establish and maintain a positive "team" relationship with parents and keep the lines of communication open.

XI. Revision

These long-range plans are by no means permanent. They may be revised and updated as necessary to meet the needs of students.

XII. List of Attachments

Attachment A: Personal Profile Sheet
Attachment B: Learning Style Assessment/Student Interest Survey
Attachment C: Weekly Progress Report
Attachment D: Daily Behavior Sheet
Attachment E: Sample Classroom Newsletter
Attachment F: Interim Progress Report

FIGURE 3.1   Teachers Planning

SAMPLE PRIMARY LONG-RANGE PLAN

I. Description of Students

I teach kindergarten at Anywhere Elementary School. My class is made up of thirty students. I have twelve African American males, one Hispanic male, four Caucasian males, six Caucasian females, and seven African American females. There are twenty-one students on free lunch and two students on reduced lunch. This tells me that many of the children come from poor homes and might need special accommodations to help them learn.

I have an ESL student and one student in developmental therapy who leaves every day at noon (except on Thursday when his developmental therapist comes for inclusion for the last hour of the day). I have two students who are being served by the speech therapist twice a week, for a total of sixty minutes per week. There is one child who has a hearing impairment and a speech impairment. She is being tested at the present time, so she can eventually receive the help that she needs to succeed and feel confident.

Using this information, I will adjust my lessons to facilitate the different needs of children in my kindergarten class. I will ask for parent and community volunteers to come and help in my classroom both to give children more individual help and to let poor parents, who might not have had a good school experience themselves, know that school is a good place to be. Also, I plan on using centers a great deal because I can change the materials to meet a wide range of ability levels and to teach a number of concepts at the same time. Centers can give bright children a challenge and low-achieving children extra practice on basic skills. This student description tells me that the long-range plan will have to include many units that build language and reinforce early learning concepts that the children in my class may have missed in their home experiences.

II. Long-Range Goals for Students

Affective Goals:

1. Students will develop a positive self-regard and build a sense of self-confidence.
2. Students will feel confident in taking risks and making choices.
3. Students will develop respect for classroom materials.
4. Students will interact easily with one or more children when playing or working cooperatively.

Academic Goals:

1. Students will perform tasks involving fine and gross motor skills.
2. Students will be able to remember visual and auditory stimuli.
3. Students will be able to determine likenesses and differences of visual and auditory stimuli.
4. Students will show an interest in language and use language to communicate with others.
5. Students will practice classifying, sequencing, and comparison skills.
6. Students will begin to understand the concept of conservation.

III. Rationale Statement

The reason for these long-range plans is to build a framework of ways to achieve the goals and objectives stated by the S.C. Education Department and the Charleston County School District for Kindergarten.

My lessons will reflect accommodations for the eight multiple intelligences (Dr. Howard Gardner). This will facilitate the different learning styles among my students. Also, I will use the six levels of Bloom's taxonomy in making my lessons. These different questioning levels will encourage higher-order thinking among the children.

During the first days of school, I will give the students an interest inventory. Then, I will tape-record the results, since the children are not writing yet. I will repeat this procedure at the end of the year to see if there have been significant developmental changes and changes in the quality of the answers. I can also share the results at the end of the year with the first-grade teachers to help their planning for the next year.

I will use thematic instruction to teach the eighteen county kindergarten objectives. During the thematic units, I will use aspects of the Cunningham reading model, which is being implemented in the school, especially in the area of language (word walls). Also, my language instruction will use language experience and lots of children's literature to build speaking and listening skills.

Mathematics concepts will be taught using manipulatives related to the unit themes; science will be taught by using a hands-on methodology that makes instruction more real for these young children. Social studies will be integrated into the theme units and will draw on children's books to do so.

Instruction will consist of whole-group and small-group instruction, with emphasis on small groups and centers. Overall, I will structure lessons and activities during the year that meet my goals, both academic and affective.

IV. Verification for the LRP

The following documents were used to verify this LRP:

Charleston County Kindergarten Objectives
South Carolina Language Arts Framework (K–3)
South Carolina Mathematics Framework (K–3)
South Carolina Science Framework (K–3)
NAEYC Guidelines for Developmentally Appropriate Practices

V. Units of Instruction _____

  A. Farm Animals (February 9–March 9)
  B. Weather (March 10–April 10)
  C. Transportation (April 11–May 11)

Activities and lessons from each unit will correlate with the nineteen kindergarten objectives used in our school district. 1. To read this schedule, one should cross-reference the kindergarten objective from the addendum with the appropriate number. For example: K.O. #1 has to do with gross motor skills development.

A. Farm Animal Unit

Week #1—Concepts: Different Types of Farm Animals (dogs, chickens, cows, pigs, sheep, horses, ducks)
K.O. #1: Students will use large muscles to move like the animals.
K.O. #2: Students will draw and paint the animals and construct art projects that involve animal names and concepts.
K.O. #3 & 4: Students will verbally compare likenesses and differences among animals.
K.O. #5: Students will recite songs and poems with animal themes and sounds.
K.O. #6: Students will discriminate the sounds of the different animal names by focusing on beginning consonant and vowel sounds.
K.O. #7 & 8: Students will use language to communicate about the different types of animals.
K.O. #9: Students will be introduced to different types of literature (stories, fables, poems) about farm animals.
K.O. #10 & 11: Students will compare and classify the animals into groups.
K.O. #12: Students will sequence patterns using farm animal manipulatives.
K.O. #13 & 14: Students will use inference skills to understand stories about farm animals.
K.O. #15 & 18: These skills will be practiced throughout the unit through cooperative learning activities.

Week #2—Concepts: Animal Sounds
K.O. #1: Students will use large muscles to move and follow commands using the sounds made by animals.
K.O. #3 & 4: Students will associate the appearance of the animal with the sound that it makes.
K.O. #5 & 6: Students will practice discriminating the different animal sounds.
K.O. #7, 8, & 9: Students will use expressive language to repeat animal sounds and names.
K.O. #10 & 11: Students will verbally compare and contrast animal sounds.
K.O. #12: Students will sequence sound patterns through songs and poems.
K.O. #13 & 14: Students will practice inference and comprehension skills through listening to and responding to animal stories.
K.O. #15 & 18: These skills will be developed through the units by cooperative learning and socialization activities.

Week #3—Concepts: Animals Move and Use Their Bodies
K.O. #1: Students will use gross and fine motor skills in animal-themed games.
K.O. #2: Students will create art projects with animal movement themes.
K.O. #3 & 4: Students will compare and contrast animal movements through visual discrimination activities.
K.O. #5 & 6: Students will practice visual discrimination by completing letter recognition activities using animal sound words.
K.O. #7 & 9: Students will use expressive language to talk about animal movements.

K.O. #10 & 11: Students will classify and compare animal movements.

K.O. #12: Students will sequence animal movements through games and pictures.

K.O. #13: Students will practice higher-order thinking skills by responding to questions about animal movements.

K.O. #15 & 18: These skills will be strengthened by daily practice in a positive learning environment.

Week #4—Concepts: Animal Homes and Habitats

K.O. #1: Students will use gross and fine motor movements to imitate animals in their natural and man-made homes.

K.O. #2: Students will use art materials to design pictures of animal homes.

K.O. #3 & 4: Students will use posters and pictures to practice visual discrimination of animal habitats.

K.O. #5 & 6: Students will complete auditory memory and auditory discrimination activities involving initial consonant sounds as they apply to animal homes and habitats.

K.O. #7 & 9: Students will be introduced to stories and poems about animal homes and will use language to communicate what they have learned. Daily journal writing begins.

K.O. #10 & 11: Students will practice sequencing skills using manipulatives and pictures involving the animal habitat theme.

K.O. #13: Students will practice number conservation by doing math activities related to animal homes.

K.O. #14: Students will use higher-order thinking skills to respond to questions about animal habitats.

K.O. #15 & 18: These skills will be improved by daily practice and individualized instruction.

B. Weather Unit

1st 7-Day Duration of Instruction—Concepts: Weather Types (cold, hot, dry, wet, calm, windy, sunny, cloudy)

K.O. #1: Students will use gross motor movements and music to act out types of weather.

K.O. #2: Students will do art projects on weather-related words and themes.

K.O. #3 & 4: Students will use visual discrimination skills to point out differences in weather.

K.O. #5 & 6: Students will practice initial consonant and vowel sounds in weather words.

K.O. #7 & 9: Students will be introduced to books about weather and will use verbal and written forms of communication.

K.O. #10 & 11: Students will compare and contrast weather.

K.O. #12: Students will use sequencing skills to respond to stories about weather.

K.O. #14: Students will use inference and observation skills to answer questions about science experiments.

K.O. #15 & 18: These skills will be reinforced through daily practice.

2nd 7-Day Duration of Instruction—Concepts: Seasons

K.O. #1: Students will use movements and music to act out scenes from the four seasons.

K.O. #2: Students will create pictures about the four seasons.

K.O. #3 & 4: Students will use visual discrimination and visual memory to respond to pictures of the four seasons.

K.O. #5 & 6: Students will use auditory discrimination and auditory memory to answer questions about the four seasons.

K.O. #7 & 9: Students will be encouraged to use language to communicate verbally and in writing about the changing seasons. Students will be introduced to literature about the seasons.

K. O. #10 & 11: Students will compare and classify differences in weather among the four seasons.

K.O. #12: Students will sequence the four seasons.

K.O. #14: Students will use inference skills by telling stories about how weather changes during the four seasons.

K.O. #15 & 18: These skills will be practiced throughout the unit by cooperative learning activities and centers, reinforced by the teacher's maintaining a positive classroom environment.

3rd 7-Day Duration of Instruction—Concepts: Weather Influences on People's Clothes and Activities

K.O. #1: Students will practice dressing for different types of weather.

K.O. #2: Students will complete art projects that focus on colors and types of clothing.

K.O. #3 & 4: Students will use visual memory to determine what types of clothes match different types of weather.

K.O. #5 & 6: Students will use beginning sounds to match the beginning letters of clothing words.

K.O. #7 & 9: Students will communicate orally and in writing about types of clothing for different weather.

K.O. #10 & 11: Students will compare and classify clothing.

K.O. #12: Students will sequence patterns of fabrics.

K.O. #13: Students will practice the concept of number conservation by using items of clothing.

K.O. #14: Students will use inference skills to answer questions about clothing and weather drawn from stories.

K.O. #15 & 18: These skills will be practiced in centers and teacher-directed activities.

C. Transportation Unit

1st 7-Day Duration of Instruction—Concepts: Water Transportation (boats, ships, submarines, jet skis)

K. O. #1: Students will use large muscles to act out the movements of water vehicles.

K.O. #2: Students will use art materials to design a form of water transportation.

K.O. #3 & 4: Students will use visual memory to identify types of water vehicles.

K.O. #5 & 6: Students will use auditory memory and discrimination to match types of water transportation to their use.

K.O. #7 & 9: Students will use language orally and in writing to communicate about water transportation. Students will be introduced to literature about water and water transportation.

K.O. #10 & 11: Students will classify and compare types of water transportation.

K.O. #12: Students will use sequencing skills to make up stories about water transportation and will make patterns using water transportation manipulatives.

K.O. #13: Students will practice the concept of conservation using water vehicle manipulatives.

K.O. #14: Students will use interpretation and inference skills to answer questions about stories involving water transportation.

K.O. #15 & 18: These skills will be used to enhance positive social interaction among children.

2nd 7-Day Duration of Instruction—Concepts: Air Transportation (planes, helicopters, hot air balloons)

K.O. #1: Students will use gross and fine motor skills to imitate the movements of aircraft.

K.O. #2: Students will use art materials to make creative pictures of aircraft.

K.O. #3 & 4: Students will use visual memory and discrimination to identify different aircraft and their uses.

K.O. #5 & 6: Students will use auditory memory and discrimination to identify different aircraft and their uses.

K.O. #7 & 9: Students will use language to communicate verbally and in writing about types of aircraft and will be introduced to stories, songs, and poems about air transportation.

K.O. #10 & 11: Students will compare and contrast types of aircraft.

K.O. #12: Students will practice sequencing skills by using stories, songs, and poems about air transportation.

K.O. #14: Students will use higher-order thinking skills to make up stories about aircraft.

K.O. #15 & 18: These skills will be used to build positive cooperative relationships among children.

3rd 7-Day Duration of Instruction—Concepts: Land Transportation (cars, trucks, motorcycles)

K.O. #1: Students will use movements to act like land vehicles.

K.O. #2: Students will use art materials to draw, paint, and design vehicles.

K.O. #3 & 4: Students will use visual memory and discrimination to name land vehicles and their uses.

K.O. #5 & 6: Students will use auditory memory and discrimination to identify and mimic the sounds of vehicles during use.

K.O. #7 & 9: Students will use language to talk about vehicles and their uses in the real world.

K.O. #10 & 11: Students will classify the shapes, sizes, and uses of vehicles.

K.O. #12: Students will sequence stories about vehicles.

K.O. #13: Students will practice the concept of number conservation by using land transportation manipulatives.

K.O. #14: Students will use higher-order thinking skills to make up stories about how they would use vehicles in a job.

K.O. #15 & 16: These skills will be used to teach children to work together and share materials in the classroom.

VI. Instructional Materials and Resources for the Units

The following materials will be used to fulfill the academic goals. The majority of materials will be found in the school. Other materials will be brought in by parents or by me. I will also use outside resources such as speakers, parents, and field trips to correlate with the units.

VCR	center tags	dress-up clothes	construction paper	crayons
glue	puppet stage	Play Doh	puzzles	writing paper
easel	blocks	big books	stamps	craft sticks
pictures	paint brushes	center chart	calendar	hot plate
paint	beans scissors	puppets	smocks	balls
dry erase board	TV	yarn	tape	magazines
clock	checklists	theme books	weather felt	
transportation felt	seasonal felt	stuffed animals	cutouts	
cutouts	cutouts	rocking chair	apple cutouts	
number line	rulers	markers		

VII. Assessment

Portfolio assessment will be used in my kindergarten. The portfolio for each child will contain anecdotal records, running records, checklists, and samples of children's work. There will also be audiotapes, videotapes, and pictures to show parents how children are learning and growing.

Anecdotal records will be taken throughout each unit and will be dated and added to the portfolio for documentation. A formal checklist of skills will be completed for each unit. Running records will be taken as needed. I will invite parents in for a portfolio conference at the end of each unit, and more often when needed. I will send home a copy of the checklists with specific comments if parents cannot come in for the end-of-unit conferences.

For my own record keeping, I will keep a whole-class checklist so that I can see, at a glance, who has mastered each skill. The following assessment tools are attached as addenda:

County Kindergarten Checklist
Teacher/Family Conversation Record
Anecdotal Record Form
Whole-Class Kindergarten Checklist
Contents of Early Childhood Portfolio Form

VIII. Student Records

Portfolios will be assessed at the end of each unit. Parents are invited to come in for conferences at the end of each unit. The parents will be given a copy of the checklists and comments to review, sign, and return to the teachers. During conferences, I will discuss strengths and weaknesses with the parents and record these on conference forms, along with our mutual ideas for enrichment and remediation.

IX. Discipline Policy

Students are expected to abide by class rules. These rules are listed in the handbook. The parents are sent a letter by the school administration, requesting that parents sign the rules after reading them.

In my classroom, I will use a behavior bulletin board titled "Keep the Worms Out of Your Apple!" Each child has a pocket shaped like an apple, with his or her name on it. The worms are painted on craft sticks. Each student starts the day out with a worm-free apple. Misbehavior earns worms:

1st worm—warning
2nd worm—10-minute loss of center time
3rd worm—loss of all center time
4th worm—parent contact
5th worm—principal's office

Students who keep their apples worm-free all week will earn a treat on Friday.

X. Procedures for Noninstructional Activities

1. *Morning Activities:* Students come in, hang up coats and bags, and sit on the carpet for a story.
2. *Bathroom:* Students may go to the classroom bathroom as needed and do not need to ask permission.
3. *Signed Papers:* There is a bin on my desk in which signed papers can be placed.
4. *Fire, Tornado, Earthquake Drills:* No talking during drills. Students are to line up by table and follow the practiced procedures.
5. *School Assemblies:* Good manners are expected during assemblies and in the school hallways. The apple behavior system will be used for these situations.
6. *Field Trips:* Good manners are expected during field trips. Serious misbehavior on a trip will result in a phone call to parent.

XI. Parent Communication

1. *Introductory Letter:* This letter will introduce me to the parents. It will outline what their children will be learning during the year. The letter will discuss the behavior policy and school supplies, as well as how they can contact me. This letter also contains an invitation to the Open House.
2. *Phone Calls:* Phone calls will be made for positive and negative reasons. I will call parents periodically during the year, to let them know how their children are doing.
3. *Conferences:* Conferences will be scheduled at the end of each unit, and more often as needed or requested by parents.
4. *Progress Reports:* Copies of the checklist and comments sheet for each unit will be given to the parent at the end of the unit; one copy is kept in the student portfolio.

Revisions: These long-range plans may be revised and adjusted as necessary to meet the needs of the students and will be kept on file for review by parents or administrators.

CHAPTER 4

Designing Short-Range (or Unit) Plans

Teaching is highly personal—an intensely intimate encounter.
The rhythm of teaching involves a complex journey, a journey of
discovery and surprise, disappointment and fulfillment. A first
step is becoming the student to your students; uncovering the
fellow creatures who must be partners to your enterprise.
(musings of William Ayers, writing in *To Teach: The Journey of a Teacher*)

It is important to begin this section with the definition of the short-range plan:

> The short-range plan (SRP) is a collection of daily lessons connected by a common theme or an integrated set of concepts. The SRP is directly related to the long-range plan (LRP) and may unfold over two to three days or two to three weeks, or longer.

Short-range plans have been called many names. You may recognize one of these as your favorite:

- Unit plan
- Integrated unit
- Project method
- Theme study
- Research project
- Literature-based unit
- Integrated study

By any name, the short-range plan is a collection of daily plans that are designed to move the curriculum along to a particular point. In this section, you will (1) review the parts of a short-range plan, (2) learn techniques for designing creative SRPs, and (3) take a look at a model SRP.

Philosophy or Rationale Statement or Purpose for the Study

List of Objectives with Verification of the Content

Resource and Materials List for the Unit

A Web or Theme Planning Matrix

Daily Lesson Plans for Each Subject Area

Assessment Plan or Posttest for the SRP

Optional: School-to-Work Statement, Parent Communication,
Children's Book List, Field Trip and Speaker List, Technology Plan

FIGURE 4.1   What's in an SRP?

HOW DO YOU PULL THE SRP FROM THE LRP?

The LRP to SRP to daily plan relationship can be considered from the perspective of courtship and marriage. The LRP is something of a fantasy. It is like dating the ideal person. One dreams about it, imagining all the romantic interludes and magical moments.

Then one gets engaged. That is the SRP stage. One begins to face reality. One must decide how long this engagement will go on and whether the intended is working out. There are details about the wedding to negotiate, and lots of phone calls to make the arrangements.

Following this metaphor, the daily plan is the bliss of married life. It gets kind of messy and tired. It takes a lot of work to keep it going and a lot of imagination to keep the parties interested. Daily plans are directly related to the LRP courtship period, but sometimes it is hard to remember that once the infatuation wears off!

Thinking Hint

✓ The long-range plan is a courtship period. Dream about your wonderful future.

✓ The short-range plan means making a commitment to the curriculum. You are engaged.

✓ The daily plan is marriage to the concepts. There is no turning back. It requires hard work and flexibility, just like any worthwhile relationship.

STEPS IN DESIGNING A SHORT-RANGE PLAN

Listed below are some areas to cover as you create your short-range plan:

❑ Review the long-range plan and pull concepts that "go together" or that you want to "teach together" under the umbrella of a theme or piece of literature.

❑ Your notes _____

_____

❑ Identify the verification statements that support your decision to teach those concepts. Use the verification information that you cited from the LRP, but be more specific. Give page numbers and/or quotes.

❑ Your notes _____

_____

❑ Formulate a brief rationale statement or "plan for the unit." Explain what you want the children to know and learn.

❑ Your notes _____

_____

❑ Use a planning matrix to brainstorm lessons and/or activities that deliver content. See pages 89 and 91.

❑ Your notes _____

_____

❏ Write lesson plans (See Chapter 5 for directions for writing daily plans).

❏ Your notes _____

_____

❏ Create a pre–post test and an assessment plan for the unit.

❏ Your notes _____

_____

❏ Draft a list of materials and resources and design other elements, such as a technology plan or school-to-work plan, as desired.

❏ Your notes _____

_____

Common Concerns about SRP Design

1. Question: How do I estimate the duration of a set of lessons?

   Possible answers:

   • Ask more experienced teachers.

   • Count on two to three days for new material and one day for review.

   • Overplan by one day.

   • It depends on how many concepts you build into the plan.

2. Question: Where do I find outside resources to support the concepts?

   Possible answers:

   • College and university faculty

   • Teacher magazines

   • The Internet

   • Parents

   • Museums and galleries

   • Library

   • Professional books on units and themes

3. Question: How many daily lesson plans does it take to make a short-range plan or unit?

   Possible answers:

   • As many as you want or have time for

   • Enough to thoroughly teach and review the concepts

   • Enough to add up to an assessment checkpoint

   • Enough to address the various learning styles and multiple intelligences found among your students

   • Two to three plans per key or major concept presented

4. Question: What is the difference between a short-range plan and a daily lesson plan?

   Possible answers:

- A short-range plan is a unified set of daily plans.

- A short-range plan is integrated, while a daily plan is isolated.

- A short-range plan takes place over a period of days or weeks, while a daily plan takes thirty minutes to a few hours to complete.

5. Question: Does a short-range plan have to be so complicated, with all the parts described in this chapter?

   Possible answers:

- No, you can simply do a set of objectives and a planning matrix.

- No, you can simply write a set of goals and gather daily plans under those goals.

- Yes, the best way to make sure that your goals from the LRP are met is to design a robust SRP.

- Yes, but you can delete those parts that you don't feel compelled to use because your skill level and expertise give you more latitude.

6. Question: Can short-range plans be modified like LRPs are modified?

   Possible answers:

- Yes, SRPs are working documents.

- Yes, SRPs should reflect your ongoing assessment. If the assessment shows that you need to spend more time on a concept, then add lessons.

- Yes, SRPs change to match the pace, needs, and interests of students.

- Yes, you might want to expand a set of concepts because you are having a marvelous time and so are the students.

Your Notes on SRPs _____

_____

_____

_____

_____

_____

_____

_____

_____

FIGURE 4.2 Moving from the LRP to the SRP

⟹ Use this page to list a variety of SRPs that might flow out of your long-range plan.

1.

Theme _____   Content Areas _____

Duration _____   Notes _____

_____

_____

2.

Theme _____   Content Areas _____

Duration _____   Notes _____

_____

_____

3.

Theme _____   Content Areas _____

Duration _____   Notes _____

_____

_____

4.

Theme _____   Content Areas _____

Duration _____   Notes _____

_____

_____

Thinking Hint: *What do you believe about units? How many myths about units have you subscribed to? What do you think now? How will this affect your planning? Here are ten common myths about units or theme-based plans:*

1. Units must fit a "cute" theme in which everything matches. This is not true. Units should naturally fit together and make sense.

2. Units must include every subject area. This is also not true. Good units can include just two subject areas, such as math and science. Or, a good unit might be one subject area, such as history, under the theme of W.W. II or Women's Studies.

3. Units have to take weeks or months to be valid. The duration of an SRP or unit is negotiable. The two- to three-day mini-unit can be a great curriculum boost.

4. A chapter in a textbook can be a unit. Not so! A chapter can be part of a unit, but a unit requires outside resources and supporting materials to add depth.

5. Creative arts are only part of early childhood units. No way! Multiple intelligences require lots of hands-on, musical, and spatial opportunities at every grade level. Besides, the arts make units fun.

6. Units or SRPs are harder to assess. I won't be able to use traditional tests. Don't worry. A unit can be assessed with both traditional tests (pull out a strand of content) and with authentic measures. In fact, I recommend both.

7. SRPs have to take a long time and be complex. I'll be overwhelmed. You worry needlessly. SRPs save you time because you "kill two birds with one stone," by planning experiments, exercises, and speakers who enrich or reinforce several objectives at one time.

8. Unit teaching is for rich schools. We don't have much as it is. Not so! Units enable you to use "found materials" and "free materials" as much as possible. Units are the consignment store of curriculum design.

9. Unit teaching will drive down test scores because we won't cover enough material. Covering material isn't teaching. The kids don't know it just because you covered it. With units, there is a better chance that the learner will internalize the content and thereby do better on a test.

10. Units are for experienced teachers. Units require a knowledge of the content, so experienced teachers should review the verification and objectives of a new teacher's unit. But novices often have the right attitude and enthusiasm for a unit. That's why teams are great for unit teaching.

TWENTY-FOUR FRESH IDEAS FOR SHORT-RANGE PLANS

Try to be imaginative as you create SRPs. Put a checkmark by those concepts below that appeal to you. Then, turn to pages 89 and 91 and use the Planning Matrix to begin brainstorming lessons for the plan. Here are some fresh ideas for unit or short-range plan themes:

1. Energy Everywhere—a study of light, heat, and sound energy

2. The Story of History—a unit that uses historical children's fiction as the basis for lessons in American history

3. Punctuation Power—a unit that emphasizes writing skills in science, social studies, and mathematics

4. Cooking Connections—a unit that showcases weekly cooking lessons that connect math and science concepts

5. Look through the Telescope and What Do You See?—a unit on basic astronomy and the lives of male and female scientists and astronauts

6. Picturing Math—a unit that teaches math skills by using Polaroid cameras

7. Peeling Back Time—a unit that uses math, science, and history concepts built around the theme of layers of the earth's crust and earth history

8. Toy Time—a unit on basic physics, including force, energy, motion, and simple machines, that uses children's toys as the connection

9. The Mailbox—a unit on letter-writing skills and geography that involves writing to pen pals around the country

10. Researchers on the Loose—a unit on teaching basic research skills by investigating world geography (a trip around the world)

11. Wise Buys—a math and social studies unit on money, banking, saving and earning, trade, and economics

12. Art-rageous—a unit that introduces children to the great masters of art and music while learning map and globe skills by studying their countries of origin

13. What's My Style?—a unit that teaches children to understand their personal style of learning, along with a health/science strand on the brain and nervous system

14. Geo-Centered Learning—a unit on the six National Geography Standards that focuses on the United States

15. Body Trek—a unit on the human body with emphasis on the systems and individual differences

16. It's about Time—a time and measurement unit, with a strand on communication skills that involves learning to use calendars, appointment books, and e-mail to keep up-to-date

17. Manners Matter—a unit on learning to use good manners at home, at school, and in society, with a geography strand on good manners in other cultures

18. That's My Baby—an environmental science unit on animal mothers and babies and their feeding habits and living habitats

19. Boulder Me Over—an earth science unit on rocks and minerals, with a social studies emphasis on the geographic location of deposits and the use of natural resources in trade and industry

20. Off to Work We Go—a unit on careers and the "soft skills" that workers need to be successful in any workplace

21. Multiplication Madness—a unit on the use of the multiplication tables in everyday life, with a strand on memorizing the tables

22. Written By—a unit on book publishing in which every child writes and publishes a book based on a science or social studies theme

23. Color by Number—a preschool unit on colors, numbers, and shapes

24. Currently Speaking—a unit that uses the newspaper to study important events and tracks these events by using world maps and other social studies resources

Your Ideas for Short-Range Plans

_____

_____

_____

_____

_____

Thinking Hint: *This is a planning matrix for the elementary grades. Use it to brainstorm lessons or concepts for your SRP.*

FIGURE 4.3 Planning Matrix—Elementary

Theme:	Language Arts	Arts	Science	Geography	Social Studies	Math	Affective Skills
Knowledge and Concepts to Learn							
Hands-On Activities							
Trips or Speakers (Special Resources)							
Children's Books or Magazines							
Technology							
Building Creativity							
Drill and Practice of Skills							
Higher-Order Thinking Skills							
Careers and the Real World							

Thinking Hint: *This is a planning matrix for the primary grades. Use it to brainstorm activities and lessons for your kindergarten or first-grade SRP.*

FIGURE 4.4   Planning Matrix—Primary

Theme:	Speech	Listening	Counting and Sorting	Concept Building	Gross Motor Skills	Fine Motor Skills	Social Skills	Problem Solving and Reasoning	Science and Geography
Music and Singing									
Books and Print Materials									
Manipulatives									
Games									
Centers									
Outdoor Play									
Five Senses									

USING THE PLANNING MATRICES EFFECTIVELY

The two planning matrices (elementary and primary) are for use in brainstorming the short-range plan. Here are some tips for using the matrices:

- ❑ Write in pencil.
- ❑ Consult the LRP to review the goals and schedule.
- ❑ Consider holidays and celebrations that might be going on during the SRP period.
- ❑ Think about what you have learned about your students and how the SRP might serve their interests and talents.
- ❑ Balance the boxes on the matrix. Try to include at least one activity or concept in each box.
- ❑ Jot down different activities in each box.
- ❑ Feel free to get rid of activities and write in new ones.
- ❑ Consider planning with a team. Ask a "musical" team member to take responsibility for the musical boxes. Get the math genius in your group to pull together some strong math lessons for the SRP. Pool your team's talents to complete the matrix.
- ❑ Look at teaching magazines or Web sites to get ideas for the matrix.
- ❑ Can you bring in parents' talents for the SRP?
- ❑ Recognize that the boxes on the matrix should turn into daily plans.

LOOKING AHEAD TO CHAPTERS FIVE AND SIX

The daily lesson plans, which are incorporated into the SRPs, are covered in detail in Chapter Five. Directions for writing daily plans, with good objectives, procedures, use of materials, and assessment, are found in Chapter Five.

In Chapter Six, you will have the opportunity to review a sample short-range or unit plan. The elementary plan was designed by Mrs. Kenya Ferguson, whose study of dinosaurs reflects her interest in science and the natural world. Notice how the plan includes both a traditional test and a set of authentic assessment tasks, with rubrics and expectations for student performance. In short-range planning, it is ideal to design the assessment when you design the unit, so that you teach what will be tested.

Also, notice how the short-range objectives and the daily plans fulfill *both* the state science objectives and the recommended concepts to be introduced at the particular grade level. Take a look at the verification statements to see how she did this.

Also, notice how the teacher incorporated her own style in the daily lesson plans but managed to include important teaching methods and procedures that made the content robust and the activities child-centered.

So, keep in mind that your models for *both the SRP and daily plans* are located in Chapter Six. Wrapping up, remember that looking at sample plans can help you to:

- Visualize the format for unit plans.

- Understand how rationale and verification statements help you in planning.

- Get a sense of how personal style and interests figure into planning.

- Appraise the application of issues such as pacing.

- See how children's learning styles can be worked into procedures.

- Grasp the concepts of integrating subject areas under a common theme.

- Think about how you might design short-range plans using themes that interest you.

- Analyze the way that teachers plan for shorter periods of instruction.

- Consider the use of assessment in short-range planning.

CHAPTER 5

Designing Daily Lesson Plans

*Everything that happens to me is according to a plan I've
been working on for years, a plan audacious in scope yet bold
in its simplicity. Everything you see me do is but a necessary
stage in the completion of this grand design.*

(Joe Robert Kirkman, the rural North Carolina teacher who is the protagonist
in Fred Chappell's novel about teaching, *Brighten the Corner Where You Are*)

Whether you see yourself as mapping out a bold and audacious plan, like the inspired Mr. Kirkman, or simply trying to get through each day with a feeling of order and satisfaction, learning to design practical, complete daily plans is an important skill. Therefore, in this chapter, we will (1) review the steps for designing daily plans, (2) identify techniques for incorporating a variety of accommodations into daily plans, and (3) look at some sample plans that have been included as part of the model unit.

Before we begin framing a daily plan, consider the purpose for creating daily lesson plans. Daily plans should be more than notations in a planning book. Daily plans should help the teacher to "plan for robust instruction" and to "individualize instruction to meet the unique needs of students." The energy that you put into thinking about and writing about the description of students back in the LRP comes to life in the daily plans:

- The daily plan is a set of directions for the day.

- The daily plan is a page of prompts for instruction.

- The daily plan can be simple or complex.

- The daily plan should contain some form of objectives, procedures, and guidelines for assessment.

- The daily plan can be scripted, checked off, or done in note form to meet your style and time constraints.

Steps for Writing a Daily Plan

- Select an objective for the lesson.

- Estimate a duration for the instructional period.

- Verify the objective for content and grade appropriateness.

- Consider the place of the objective in terms of what you have already taught and assessed (i.e., Is this the right objective today?).

- Create activities and procedures to help students meet that objective.

- Formulate a materials and resource list to match the procedures.

- Design an assessment to let you know if the children have mastered the objective and to let the children know what they have learned.

- Think about how this lesson will help the children fulfill some of the goals set forth in the SRP and, ultimately, the LRP (i.e., Is this lesson timely, necessary, and part of my academic plan for the year?).

Write your questions about the steps for daily plans here.

_____

_____

_____

_____

_____

Will you need to make your daily plans more detailed?

_____

_____

FIGURE 5.1   Outline for Daily Plan

Teacher _____   Grade Level _____   Duration of Instruction _____

Objective: The students will _____
_____
_____
_____
_____

Verification: This lesson is supported by _____
_____
_____

Rationale: This lesson is critical because_____
_____
_____

Procedures: _____
_____

  1. (Introduction of objective and review of prior learning)_____
     _____
  2. _____
     _____
  3. _____
     _____
  4. _____
     _____
  5. _____
     _____
  6. _____
     _____
  7. _____
     _____

  8. (Support for special needs) _____
     _____

  9. (Enrichment) _____
     _____

 10. (Wrap up and review; link to next lesson)_____
     _____

Materials and Resources Needed: _____
_____
_____

Assessment of Objective:_____
_____
_____

FIGURE 5.2   Outline for Daily Plan

Teacher _____   Grade Level _____   Duration of Instruction _____

Objective: The students will _____

_____

_____

_____

Verification: This lesson is supported by _____

_____

Rationale: This lesson is critical because_____

_____

Procedures: _____

_____

  1. (Introduction of objective and review of prior learning)_____

  2. _____

  3. _____

  4. _____

  5. _____

  6. _____

  7. _____

  8. (Support for special needs) _____

  9. (Enrichment) _____

 10. (Wrap up and review; link to next lesson)_____

Materials and Resources Needed: _____

_____

Assessment of Objective:_____

_____

FIGURE 5.3 Outline for Daily Plan

Teacher _____ Grade Level _____ Duration of Instruction _____

Objective: The students will _____

_____

_____

_____

_____

Verification: This lesson is supported by _____

_____

_____

Rationale: This lesson is critical because_____

_____

_____

Procedures: _____

_____

1. (Introduction of objective and review of prior learning)_____

   _____

2. _____

   _____

3. _____

   _____

4. _____

   _____

5. _____

   _____

6. _____

   _____

7. _____

   _____

8. (Support for special needs) _____

   _____

9. (Enrichment) _____

   _____

10. (Wrap up and review; link to next lesson)_____

    _____

Materials and Resources Needed: _____

_____

_____

Assessment of Objective:_____

_____

_____

FIGURE 5.4   Shortcut Model for Daily Plan*

Day _____   Grade _____   Unit _____

Objectives for the day

_____
_____
_____
_____
_____

Activities for the day that meet the objectives

_____
_____
_____
_____
_____
_____

Special materials needed for today that are not found in my classroom

_____
_____
_____

Will any students require enrichment or accommodations in order to participate fully in today's lessons? If so, explain here:

_____
_____

Is there a test, quiz, or authentic assessment planned for today?

Yes (explain) _____

Daily planning notes/Reminders about parent conferences

*Copy these as needed, and place them in a three-ring binder or on a clipboard.

FIGURE 5.5   Matrix for Daily Planning (for use by experienced teachers)

Teacher _____ Grade _____ Week of _____

	Daily	Mon.	Tues.	Wed.	Thurs.	Fri.
Language						
Reading						
Math						
Science						
Social Studies						
Arts						
Special Needs						

Planning Notes for the Week

Parents _____

Homework _____

Tests _____

Projects _____

Forms/Field Trips _____

FIGURE 5.6   Special Accomodations for Daily Plans*

Purpose: Complete one of these sheets each week, and attach to your short-range lesson plans. This will serve as documentation for 504 plans and IEPs, well as less formal assistance to children who may be experiencing problems.

Week of _____Teacher _____Grade _____

Student _____Circle One: 504   IEP   Help Needed

Assistance Provided: _____

_____

Notes: _____

_____

Student _____Circle One: 504   IEP   Help Needed

Assistance Provided: _____

_____

Notes: _____

_____

Student _____Circle One: 504   IEP   Help Needed

Assistance Provided: _____

_____

Notes: _____

_____

Student _____Circle One: 504   IEP   Help Needed

Assistance Provided: _____

_____

Notes: _____

_____

*Reproduce these pages as needed, and put them in a three-ring binder or on a clipboard.

STARTING THE LESSON OFF RIGHT—WITH THE RIGHT OBJECTIVE!

Objectives tell you what the children should "know and be able to do" by the end of the lesson. Therefore, the objectives must contain a *measurable action word—a verb*. Avoid the use of *learn* or *understand* in objectives. Instead, choose from these verbs to create meaningful objectives. These verbs are grouped into several categories to encourage your own creativity.

To Help You

What do you think are some differences between poor and good objectives? Here are some examples of weak or poorly written objectives, followed by stronger, more sound objectives:

Weak Objectives

- Students understand the vocabulary words.

- Students know how to do three-digit addition with regrouping.

- Students learn the major landforms.

Better Objectives

- Students define the ten science vocabulary words by using them in complete sentences.

- Students solve ten problems by using three-digit addition with regrouping.

- Students identify the major landforms, including rivers, plateaus, mountains, and lakes, by pointing them out on a topographical map of the United States.

Use this space to record your observations about what makes a good objective in a daily plan.

FIGURE 5.7 Thinking about Planning

FIGURE 5.8

Language Arts	*Science*	*Mathematics*
Write	Observe	Solve
Describe	Predict	Complete
Edit	Classify	Group
Create	Compare	Measure
Tell	Show	Predict
Predict	Make	Categorize
Identify	Measure	Estimate
Restate	Give examples	Put in order
Give main idea	Investigate	Chart
Explain	Invent	Graph
Summarize	Draw	Calculate
Tell why	Tell when	Tell how
Discuss	Dissect	Diagram
Propose	Formulate	Demonstrate
Plot	Prepare	Practice
Define	Detect	Determine
Translate	Trace	Track
Dramatize	Report	Graph
Relate	Hypothesize	Plan
Read	Collect	Set up

Social Studies/Geography	*Creative Arts*
Show	Create
Find	Design
Match	Make
Give	Draw
Recognize	Illustrate
Repeat	Paint
Choose	Organize
Argue	Construct
Clarify	Collect
Paraphrase	Dramatize
Demonstrate	Direct
Distinguish	Model
Debate	Evaluate
Locate	Listen and describe

Notes on Using Verbs:

- These verbs can be used in any objective that you like.

- Remember that verbs are connected to the activities; they drive the activities to varying levels of critical thinking skills. (You can make the lesson more simple or more challenging by changing the verb.)

PROCEDURES MAKE THE DAILY PLAN PROCEED AS PLANNED!

Can you say that line three times without stumbling? It is a real tongue twister, but an important concept in daily planning. Solid, clear procedures are the most helpful part of a daily plan, yet they are the part most often neglected or even ignored. Many teachers will take the time to jot down objectives and maybe a note on activities and assessment, but procedures are what teachers think they can keep in their heads. Yet, with large class sizes, a host of competing distracters, and the needs of handicapped, gifted, and troubled children to consider on a minute-by-minute basis, it is tough to keep procedures in mind, much less flowing smoothly, unless you make some effort to write them down or remind yourself of them.

Moreover, procedures in a daily plan function as your insurance policy for meeting specific learning-style needs, academic needs, and social goals for the short-range plan. Procedures make your plans work for the children and for you. On the next few pages, you will find directions for writing procedures, examples of well or poorly designed procedures, and a roster of activities for special needs students that can be incorporated into procedures.

Directions for Writing Procedures

The first procedures could include the following:

• Begin with a procedure that captures the students' attention. Sometimes, this is called a "set," a "stimulating technique," or an "opening strategy." You might use a startling statement, a rhetorical question, a video clip, a song, a prop, a (brief) experiment or demonstration, or even a children's story.

• Design a procedure that introduces the students to the daily objective and its value. Tell or show the students why they should learn or master this material or concept.

• Connect the first two procedures with past learning or a prior lesson. Use a procedure, such as questioning or an example, that allows the students to see and hear how the new lesson builds on prior knowledge.

The next procedures should incorporate various learning styles or multiple intelligences. Use as many procedures as you have time for to allow students to see, touch, smell, draw, write, manipulate, sing, or do something to make the acquisition of knowledge more interesting and real. These kinds of procedures are referred to as "learning strategies":

• Include procedures for slow learners, gifted learners, and those with disabilities. Use the form on page 115 to help you include all students. Use varying group sizes in the procedures. These procedures are referred to as "accommodations" or "inclusion strategies."

• Make sure that you develop at least one procedure for "drill and practice" of the objective. You must watch the students doing the objective, or your lesson is in vain. It is not enough to for you to talk about or refer to the objective; the students must be actively involved in the objective.

• Begin to check for understanding of the objective with procedures that check for mastery or progress in a skill or application of new knowledge. You may ask questions, give a quiz, or take a sample of student work. These procedures may be individually done, done in pairs, or done in a group. These are assessment or assessment-building procedures.

- Design a "wrapping-up" procedure. In this procedure, draw the students' attention to the next day or next lesson. Tell or show them how what they have experienced in this lesson will connect to new learning. Emphasize the usefulness of this knowledge or skill. Praise the children for their mastery and effort. Some call these procedures "closure," "recapping learning," or "review."

Use this space to outline the important steps in procedure design:

_____

_____

_____

_____

_____

_____

To Help You

Here are some examples of weak or poorly written procedures:

- Write in science journals.

- Solve problems 1–10 in math book.

- Have center time.

Now, here are the same procedures, rewritten for clarity:

- After observing the Jello-making experiment, students respond to the following prompt and record it in their science journal: "What did I learn about physical change by observing the Jello-making experiment?" Students should use at least two science vocabulary words in their statement.

- Students practice addition with regrouping by solving problems 1–10 on page 88 of the math book. ADD and LD students may solve 1–7 only. G & T students may solve 1–5 only, and then proceed to the challenge section on page 89. Students may check their answers by using calculators.

- Have forty-five minutes of center time. Each child must circulate to the handwriting table to work on writing name and phone number. The bell will ring at fifteen-minute intervals to signal a center change.

Powerful Procedures to Incorporate into Daily Plans!

Finally, this section offers procedures that help you to meet the learning needs of students who may require more specific, aggressive attention during a daily lesson. Read on to review suggested procedures that you might like to incorporate into daily plans for your classroom. The procedures are grouped by specific student needs but can be interchanged to develop creative plans of your own:

Procedures for Students with Attention Deficit Disorders

- Alternate active and passive activities.
- Pair children to complete an activity.
- Complete part of a written activity in class and save part for homework.
- Avoid distractions during instruction (visual, auditory, tactile).
- Schedule several chunks of lecture interspersed with activity.
- Make sure the work area is neat and clear before beginning a lesson.

Procedures for Students Who Do Not Speak English as Their Primary Language

- Pair the child with a buddy note taker.
- Audiotape review lessons to listen to for homework.
- Use lots of illustrations and demonstrations in the lesson.
- Speak slowly and clearly but not more loudly than usual.
- Use photography, such as an instant camera, for projects.

Procedures for Gifted Students

- Use the computer and software for individual enrichment.
- Assign the "challenge questions" in a chapter instead of the same review and practice items.
- Give the children independent research projects to work on in small groups.
- Incorporate writing often.
- Bring an artistic side into academic lessons.
- Allow the children to finish early and start a new project.
- Use the scent or taste of cinnamon or ginger to encourage creativity.

Procedures for Developmentally Delayed Students

- List the steps in a math problem or task on chart paper.
- Give more time to complete tasks.
- Use open-book tests and avoid "pop" quizzes.
- Read aloud or assign paired reading.
- Give the children neon-colored or scented markers to highlight text.
- Structure concepts from easy to complex.
- Use the scent and taste of peppermint to encourage alertness.

Procedures for Students Who Are Auditory Learners

- Verbalize steps.

- Ask frequent questions.
- Engage children in conversation or Socratic dialogue about concepts.
- Use music as a prompt or in the background during drill and practice.
- Do an oral review for tests.
- Use buddy reading.
- Use a tape recorder.
- Guard against background noise during lessons.

Procedures for Students Who Are Visual Learners

- Use laser-disc slides of science and social studies concepts.
- Give a printed chapter outline or study notes.
- Let children use a whiteboard or wipe-off board to practice spelling words.
- Color-code folders, index cards, or notes.
- Use the overhead frequently.
- Use flashcards for drill and practice.
- Teach note-taking skills to use during observations.

Procedures for Students Who Are Tactile-Kinesthetic Learners

- Use manipulatives in the lesson.
- Try cooking activities.
- Provide a spacious, clear work area that allows for freedom of movement.
- Encourage children to illustrate as well as write in journals.
- Bring in individual chalkboards and colored chalk.
- Incorporate art into lessons (collages, painting).
- Use blocks to teach math concepts.

Hints for Productive Materials Use in Daily Plans

- Materials bring the procedures to life and help students express themselves.
- Materials can enhance a lesson or result in loss of valuable instructional time.
- Materials should be organized effectively and ordered ahead of time.
- Materials should be provided for whole-group, cooperative-group, and individual use.
- Materials should be cared for by the students, and they should have a predictable, practiced system for using and putting away materials.
- Use the lists provided to brainstorm and organize the materials that you will incorporate into daily plans.

My List of Materials for Daily Whole-Group Use

Chalkboard, chalk

Whiteboard, markers

Overhead

_____

_____

_____

_____

_____

_____

_____

_____

My List of Materials for Cooperative Groups

Toolbox or basket

_____

_____

_____

_____

_____

Materials for Individual Children to Provide

_____

_____

_____

_____

_____

My Personal Materials for Teaching

Reward stickers and stars

Colored pens

Apron

_____

_____

_____

_____

_____

_____

Did You Forget?

alphabet blocks	scent pot/ potpourri	binders	calculators
string	handwriting paper	rocking chair	magazines
construction paper	posters	stamps/stickers	clay or Play Doh
scissors	blocks	pets/pet supplies	encyclopedias
yardsticks	yarn	classical music	balls and hoops
dictionaries	tinfoil	handwriting chart	certificates
audiotapes	felt	sewing kit	plants
flash cards	pencils	counters	medicine kit
textbooks	computer	rulers	bulletin board supplies
puzzles	tape or CD player	markers	tissues
soap	tape	beakers	glue
eraser	bins and boxes	crayons	writing paper
folders	cooking materials	printer	paint
sticky notes	rubber gloves	maps/globe	tin plates
graph paper	rubbing alcohol	transparencies	pencil sharpener
study corral	chart paper	beanbag	TV-VCR
stapler/staples	white-out	paper cups	science materials
storybooks	rubber bands	paper clips	shelving
candy or treats	index cards	software	paste
extension cord		pocket chart	pins

FINALLY—ASSESSMENT

In each of the sections on long-range planning, short-range planning, and daily planning, there has been a discussion of assessment. There is a reason for so much repetition—assessment is too often neglected. See if you consider assessment in these ways:

❑ Monitoring and checking to see if the objectives have been mastered by each student is necessary.

❑ Assessment is both a *process* and a *product.*

❑ We need to see, touch, and evaluate the students' progress.

❑ Assessment can be formal or informal.

❑ Assessment can be traditional or authentic.

❑ Assessment should be done constantly and carefully.

❑ Assessment should be built into every daily plan.

❑ The daily assessment should be tied to the overall assessment plan for the unit.

❏ The short-range assessment plan should be connected to the long-range plan for the year.

❏ The long-range assessment plan should flow out of the long-term goals.

❏ At least one procedure in each daily plan should contain an element of assessment.

❏ Write your interpretation of assessment in the space below:

_____

_____

_____

_____

_____

Interesting Ideas for Assessment _____

Here are some creative ways to build assessment into daily plans:

- Ask questions to a buddy.
- Make up a quiz.
- Draw a six-frame cartoon demonstrating knowledge of a concept.
- Solve problems on a worksheet, on a wipe-off board, or in a center.
- Answer review questions.
- Write a short paragraph.
- Fill in a blank map, chart, or matrix with information.
- Explain how you completed a problem.
- Show your work on the overhead or the board.
- Create an art project that illustrates the concept.
- Use the skill to solve a problem.
- Respond to a written prompt.
- Tell what you learned.
- Design a skit or commercial using the knowledge.
- Compose a song or poem using the knowledge.
- Build a model using the knowledge.
- Take a traditional test.
- Make a flip book, booklet, or brochure using the information.
- Fill in the blanks on an outline with information or vocabulary.
- Solve a challenge problem using the skill.

  Write your creative assessment ideas in Figure 5.9:

FIGURE 5.9

LET'S REVIEW

What did you learn about daily plans? Read the following checklist:

✓ Daily plans are a part of the SRP.

✓ Daily plans enable you to meet individual needs.

✓ Daily plans have a format that requires a reason for teaching the lesson.

✓ Verification helps you to pinpoint objectives that are most valuable and critical.

✓ The objective in a daily plan should be measurable and tangible.

✓ Procedures should flow from simple to abstract.

✓ Procedures should include all kinds of learners and rates of learning.

✓ Materials bring procedures to life but can rob you of instructional time if they are disorganized.

✓ Assessment can be formal or informal but should be included in every lesson.

✓ In assessment, students should show what they know!

✓ Daily plans can be organized by using a formal narrative or by jotting down notes on a form or matrix.

LOOKING AHEAD TO CHAPTER SIX

The sample daily plans are included as part of the SRP (short-range plan) in Chapter Six. Use the space on the next page to make notes on how the teachers demonstrate their skill in the following areas:

• Using verification to frame their objectives

• Writing a rationale statement that guides the lesson

- Designing measurable objectives
- Carefully planning for materials use
- Creating procedures that meet lots of learning styles and needs
- Wrapping up the lesson neatly
- Using a variety of group sizes
- Building in assessment

FIGURE 5.10 My Notes after Reviewing the Sample Plans

CHAPTER 6

Sample Short-Range and Daily Plans to Review

Form your plan before sunrise.
(Indian proverb)

Practice makes the master.
(German proverb)

Procrastination is the thief of time.
(English proverb)

As we enter the final turn in the planning journey, these proverbs give sustenance. You may be asking, Why do I need to include details such as standards, skills, and specific procedures that deliver skills? How will this help me and my students?

Detailed short-range and daily plans are like high-protein trail mix that energizes and empowers when the hiker feels faint. As you deliver instruction, it will be helpful to consult your well-structured plans in order to stay on task and to make sure that you thoroughly teach all of the skills and standards that children in your grade level and content area are required to master.

The sample plans provided in this section do contain a great deal of detail; as I explained in the introduction, not every teacher needs or wants to do this kind of detailed planning on a daily or weekly basis. However, many novice teachers, and certainly those in training, will be required to do this by their supervisors (and, due to their lack of experience, they may prefer to do this).

A WORD ABOUT LOCAL AND NATIONAL STANDARDS

In this section, you will see teachers citing state *South Carolina Frameworks* and other standards as part of the verification or rationale statements in the plans. This is part of an important national trend toward accountability. Indeed, in many states, teachers are now required to cite the state standards, state objectives, or district skills that are delivered in instruction. Moreover, new state and national testing instruments will trace student performance back to instruction and give teachers and administrators a profile of which skills were not mastered by students. It will become increasingly important to *identify specific skills, objectives, or standards,* as they are termed in your area, *on daily plans.*

DINOSAUR DETECTIVES UNIT _____

I. Rationale Statement _____

This unit was designed for a second-grade classroom at Anytown Elementary School. These students are fascinated by dinosaurs and mystified by their enormous proportions. By teaching a Dinosaur Unit, the learning that will take place will be inquiry-based. The students will be motivated to learn about these extinct creatures.

This topic has been around for some time and has become a thoroughly integrated thematic unit. None of the subjects were forced to fit into the theme; they naturally fell into place with a little creativity. The subject of dinosaurs puts emphasis on both science and social studies, which is rare but beneficial. Language arts, math, and creative arts are also heavily taught and reinforced throughout the unit. The students will be able to experience a whole-language approach to learning. This approach will maximize their learning potential because it is of high interest to them. Teaching dinosaurs encompasses a wide range of subject matter, which allows all students to find an area of enjoyment in the lessons.

All of the lesson objectives are derived from my long-range plans. These academic goals were developed in accordance with the *South Carolina Frameworks* series. The objectives are taught in the sequence followed by the prescribed basal series for Anytown County School District. The objectives are direct, logically sequenced, practiced, and reinforced with appropriate hands-on activities.

Dinosaurs only get better with age. Their mythical appeal grows, and so does the number of innovative ways to teach about them. My students will be so occupied with heuristic activities that they may not even realize that they are actually learning skills they need in life.

II. Verification _____

1. Anytown County Curriculum Guides for Language Arts, Math, and Science
2. *National Geography Standards*
3. *South Carolina Language Arts Frameworks*
4. *South Carolina Mathematics Frameworks*
5. *South Carolina Science Frameworks*
6. *South Carolina Visual and Performing Arts Frameworks*
7. *Treasury Of Literature: Sidewalk Sings* (Basal and Scope and Sequence), Harcourt Brace
8. *Destinations in Science,* Addison Wesley
9. *Houghton Mifflin Math*

III. Goals for the Unit _____

Content Goals

Language Arts

   The students will:
1. Read and be exposed to many forms of literature. (LRP Goal #4)
2. Use language in a variety of forms (listening, speaking, and writing) to strengthen communication skills. (LRP Goal #3)
3. Learn elementary grammar and phonics rules (capitalization, punctuation, and short vowel sounds) in order to improve their competence in English. (LRP Goal #2)

Math

> *The students will:*
1. Learn to identify, classify, and compare geometric shapes according to color, shape, and size. (LRP Goal #3)
2. Make and use estimates of measurement in order to measure and compare dinosaurs' proportions. (LRP Goal #4)
3. Develop a strong sense of numbers as they count, group, and sort different dinosaurs and their bones. (LRP Goal #1)

Science

> *The students will:*
1. Understand how dinosaurs interacted with their environment. (LRP Goal #1)
2. Be introduced to the processes and theories believed to have changed the dinosaurs' environments. (LRP Goal #2)
3. Learn the process of fossilization and its importance to the study of dinosaurs. (LRP Goal #2)

Social Studies

> *The students will:*
1. Be able to associate dinosaurs with their names. (LRP Goal #1)
2. Learn the names of the continents and be introduced to the theory of Pangea and continental drift by exploring where dinosaur fossils have been found. (LRP Goal #1)
3. Study how humans can learn about the past lives of dinosaurs by studying fossils. (LRP Goal #3)

Creative Arts

> *The students will:*
1. Explore movement through kinesthetic activities related to the Dinosaur Unit. (LRP Goal #1)
2. Express their personalities through artistic projects, and develop a sense of self. (LRP Goal #2)
3. Creatively use media and share their products with the class. (LRP Goal #2)

Behavioral Goals

> *The students will:*
1. Handle all materials properly and follow directions. (LRP Goal #3)
2. Obey classroom and school rules. (LRP Goal #4)
3. Participate in class activities and complete all work to the best of their ability. (LRP Goal #2)

Affective Goals

> *The students will:*
1. Interact respectfully with others in cooperative or whole-group activities. (LRP Goal #1)
2. Appreciate the dinosaurs as an ancient part of the earth's history. (LRP Goal #2)
3. Be motivated to learn about the lives of dinosaurs. (LRP Goal #2)

IV. Theme Outline

Dinosaur Detectives Discover the Mesozoic Age—"Age of the Dinosaurs"

Week 1: Fossils Make Great Clues!

Lesson Objectives:

Language Arts

1.* Initiate the students as official Dinosaur Detectives. Teach them the "Dinosaur Detective" song. Give them detective magnifying glasses. Read a few dinosaur books and do K-W-L strategy.
2. The students will read a variety of dinosaur books during sustained silent reading time. They will make words during the Word Block using the word dinosaur. They will write about the dinosaur stories during Writing Block.
3. The students will predict the animals in the *Extinct Alphabet Book* and note details about the pictures. Discuss the concept of extinction.
4. The teacher will introduce word wall words and play usage bingo, using dinosaur sentences and dinosaur bones "pasta" as the markers.
5. After reading and discussing *Digging Up Dinosaurs,* the students will write about their experience of making and digging up fossils in their journal.

Math

1. The teacher will introduce grouping according to like characteristics by having students sort the geo-dinosaur bones (colored squares, circles, rectangles, and triangles).
2. The teacher will introduce graphs and charts and discuss how they can be used. The students will make a graph of students who like dinosaurs and students who do not.
3. The class will do practice charts of various dinosaur characteristics; have students work cooperatively on them.
4. The class will review these concepts together for the remainder of the week until mastery is achieved.

Science/Social Studies

1. The teacher will explain that no humans lived when the dinosaurs or "terrible lizards" roamed the earth. The teacher will explain that what we know about dinosaurs we learn through their fossils, plant fossils, and other matter surrounding the fossils. The teacher will also discuss several myths about dinosaurs that have been shown to be false after studying fossils (e.g., not all dinosaurs were mean, large, and slow).
2. The teacher will explain the process of fossilization as minerals replacing bones as they deteriorate while keeping the shape of the bones. The students will make fossils of various objects; then in groups, they will try to figure out what each is.
3. The teacher will explain the role of a paleontologist as a Dinosaur Detective. The teacher will simulate a dig by having students dig for dinosaurs' bones and other artifacts in dried plaster of paris.
4. The students will learn the Mesozoic heroic chant. The class will read and discuss *Dinosaur Bones.*

Week 2: Triassic Period

Lesson Objectives:

Language Arts

1. Introduce dinosaurs and other related terms as unit vocabulary words; practice their meanings using 3×5 cards. The class will make predictions and read *Dazzle the Dinosaur.*

2. Explain the characteristics of Diamantes and read examples to the class. Using a dinosaur from the Triassic Period, have students write dinosaur poems and share them with the class.

3. Play What Dinosaur Am I Thinking Of? to reinforce the characteristics of each dinosaur.

4. Introduce and discuss the importance and use of ellipses, the short "a" vowel, and capitalization, Have students point them out when they read the story *If the Dinosaurs Came Back*, by Bernard Most.

5.*Have students make predictions in the story, and then do a sequencing filmstrip afterwards. Have them describe the pictures, copy the format, and paint their own event for *If the Dinosaurs Came Back*.

Math

1. The class will read and discuss *Dinosaurs Are Different* and then measure the heights of dinosaurs in the Triassic Period in small groups; have the class graph the heights, using a scale, and compare them.

2. Make a chart of students who would prefer to be plant-eaters and those who would prefer to be meat-eaters.

3. Have students measure the lengths of two of the tallest dinosaurs, compare and contrast them, and enter comparison in their journals.

4. Review and revise as necessary to ensure mastery.

Science/Social Studies

1. Introduce the Triassic Period and the dinosaurs of that time. Describe the environment at that time. Read and discuss *Do You Know How Dinosaurs Lived?*

2. Define and discuss the physical differences between plant-eaters and meat-eaters (teeth, claws, free arms, speed, etc.), and classify the Triassic dinosaurs into those categories.

3.*Have students make models of plant-eaters' and meat-eaters' mouths, and compare and contrast them in their journals.

4. The teacher will discuss the continents where dinosaur fossils have been found; have students practice map skills by locating and identifying continents.

5. Students identify dinosaurs by their descriptions, after practicing them in a memory game format.

Week 3: Jurassic Period

Lesson Objectives:

Language Arts

1. The teacher will introduce a story and vocabulary words on the Triassic or Jurassic Period. The class will set a purpose for reading the story *Mitchell Is Moving* and make predictions about the story. The teacher will reinforce the use of structural analysis and context clues as students come upon unknown words.

2. After the reading, the students will map the story in writing. The teacher will explain the use of quotation marks, dialogue words, and short "I" vowels and have students locate them in the story.

3. The class will write a chart story about their field trip to the Charleston Museum. The teacher will introduce contractions and ask children to use them in the story.

4. The teacher will have students describe the different dinosaurs and then write a play using contractions, quotations, dialogue words, and antonyms.

5. The students will practice new word wall words and use them with vocabulary words in dinosaur sentences.

6. Read and discuss *My Visit to the Dinosaurs*, by Aliki, reinforcing reading skills.

7.*The students will make and illustrate a story about a pet dinosaur.

Math

1. The class will measure dinosaur footprints found in the classroom when they got to school.
2. The teacher will introduce time telling (hours and minutes) with the students, using dinosaur characters.
3. The students will practice telling time by doing worksheets of dinosaur characters.
4. Students will write a detailed daily time schedule of events that occur in their pet dinosaur's day and then draw a picture of a clock next to each time fact that supports it (e.g., Dino the dinosaur wakes up at 6:45 A.M.).
5. Review and revise as necessary to check mastery.

Science/Social Studies

1.* Go on a field trip to the Charleston Museum where dinosaur fossils are located. Students will pick their favorite dinosaur and draw what they think it might look like over its skeleton.
2. The class will discuss the characteristics of real dinosaurs (lived on land, had legs under bodies, held tails off the ground, could not fly, were not fire-breathers). Have students do a worksheet reinforcing characteristics of real dinosaurs.
3. Go over all introduced dinosaurs; describe them and classify them as Triassic or Jurassic dinosaurs. Play memory activity.
4. Update the timeline to include Triassic and Jurassic periods under the Mesozoic Age. Have students volunteer to put the dinosaurs under the age they lived in.
5. Students will research their (museum choice) dinosaur, using the dictionary only, and make a dinosaur menu according to the information (e.g., Rex is coming to dinner so I will serve…). Have them share their menus and pictures with the class.
6. Add to the dinosaur timeline chart by classifying them as meat-eaters and plant-eaters.
7.* Have students learn the dinosaur song to reinforce characteristics about dinosaurs. Read and discuss *New Questions and Answers About Dinosaurs*.

Week 4: Cretaceous Period

Lesson Objectives:

Language Arts

1. Introduce vocabulary words, and set a purpose for reading other stories about dinosaurs by making several predictions. Discuss the use of capitalization in the story. Discuss cause and effect, and apply it to the story. Help students to use context clues and structural analysis to figure out unknown words.
2a.* Have students write "_____ Is Coming to Dinner," using time, quotation marks, and capitalization.
2b. Have students write an advertisement for a dinosaur of their choice, using capitals and noting details (review of previously learned skills).
2c. Introduce word wall words in dinosaur sentences and have students practice them. Have students use these words in their dinosaur dinner story.
3. Have students practice making words with the word "Cretaceous" during word wall. Read and discuss *A Dinosaur Ate My Homework*.
4. Students will read about or research specific dinosaurs during SSR every day.

Math

1. Read and discuss *Dinosaur Time*. Review time telling, with manipulative clocks, using dinosaur events (e.g., Dino needs to leave at 5:30; show me 5:30).
2. Review measurement and sorting by sorting dinosaurs bones pasta and then measuring them.
3. Do an update on the favorite dinosaur graph, using all dinosaurs.
4. Have students practice simple addition and subtraction on a review sheet.

5.* Have students create a dinosaur: its proportions (height, length), its daily schedule, its period, its characteristics (appearance, meat- or plant-eater), and its name. It must have the characteristics of a real dinosaur!!! Have students share with the class. Students may make a model out of any material, but it must be able to stand!

Science/Social Studies

1. Go on a field trip to Dorchester State Park; go dinosaur digging. Then have students write a journal response about the experience.
2. Complete the Cretaceous Period timeline. Classify and describe the dinosaurs of this period; reclassify them as either plant- or meat-eaters.
3. Introduce, explain, and discuss the theories related to dinosaur extinction, and have students write their own. Read and discuss *What Happened to the Dinosaurs?*
4. Play memory games with all dinosaurs and their descriptions, and then again with dinosaurs and their respective periods.
5. Add new dinosaurs to the dinosaur song. Have students sing the "Dinosaur Detective" song and chant to Mesozoic Heroic chant.

Unit Review

1. The Big D Challenge—this game uses a spelling bee format but asks review questions about the Dinosaur Unit.
2. Read *100 Dinosaurs From A to Z;* have students identify as many dinosaurs as possible.

*Creative art activity is integrated into the lesson.

V. Plan for Using Technology and School-to-Work Goals

The career field in America has shifted from desk work to contextual, hands-on work. Students are not being taught the skills they need to be qualified for the job market. Many students do not even realize how diverse the career field really is. In order to introduce students early on to the technologies and careers of today, my students will participate in these events:

- E-mail dinosaur centers for information about the dinosaurs and their lives

- Look up dinosaur information on the Internet and see if there are any virtual reality scenes.

- Watch laser-disc frames, showing students how the dinosaurs move and what the earth may have looked like at that time.

- Invite a paleontologist to come in and share some experiences and details about this line of work.

The purpose of these activities is to expose students to these fields and get them thinking about what they might like to pursue as a career. The goal of these activities is to broaden students' knowledge of the real world.

VI. Assessment Plan

In this unit, the students will be evaluated by both authentic and traditional summative assessments. Every week of the unit has a review and mastery lesson where the teacher can evaluate students' mastery, revise as necessary, and move on.

The traditional test covers knowledge and memorization of learned information. It contains matching, fill-in-the-blank, multiple-choice, and true-and-false sections. All of the questions come from lesson objectives that have been taught numerous times throughout the unit.

The authentic assessment allows the teacher to see if students can apply what they've learned. Authentic assessment enables the teacher to evaluate whether or not the students were able to make meaningful connections between the subject areas. The evaluation also allows students to demonstrate what they know in a holistic and creative context, using many modalities.

The tests will be weighted as follows:

Traditional end-of-unit test	20
Authentic summative and formative tests	25
Journal entries	5
Total possible points	50

(convert to 100-point scale by multiplying by 2)

90–100 = A; 80–89 = B; 70–79 = C; 60–69 = D; 59 and below = redo

Journal entries will be evaluated according to effort (e.g., did they try to be thorough, or did they skim through the entry?).

This assessment approach will give the teacher a fairly accurate estimate concerning the students' level of mastery and their individual learning styles. It was designed to allow students to work at their highest level throughout the unit. By varying the test formats, this assessment allows for students' individual needs.

TRADITIONAL TEST _____

Dinosaur Detectives Test _____

Fill in the correct word for each sentence. (Objectives are found in lessons.)

| lizard | extinct | Triceratops | meat-eating | Cretaceous |

1. The word dinosaur means "terrible _____." (week 1, SS 1)
2.*Dinosaurs are _____; they are no longer living on the earth. (week 1, LA 1)
3. The _____ dinosaur had three horns on its head. (week 4, SS 2; "Dinosaur Detective" song)
4.*The _____ Period is the last period in the Age of the Dinosaurs. (week 4, SS1)

Circle the answer True if it is correct or False if it is wrong.

5. Many dinosaurs had fins for swimming.   True   False
   (week 3, SS 2; week 4, M 5)
6. Humans and dinosaurs lived together.   True   False
   (week 1, SS 1)
7. Some dinosaurs could run fast.   True   False
   (week 2, SS 2)
8. The Ultrasaurus was the largest dinosaur.   True   False
   (week 2, LA 3; "Dinosaur Detective" song)
9. The Tyrannosaurus Rex was also called the "King."   True   False
   (week 4, SS 2)
10.*All dinosaurs were large and mean.   True   False
   (week 1, SS 1)

Multiple-Choice: Circle the best answer for each question.

11. Real dinosaurs had
    (week 3, SS 2; week 4, M 5)
    a. legs all over their bodies.
    b. legs directly under their bodies.
    c. legs on their backs.
    d. no legs.

12. The _____ was a meat-eating dinosaur.
    (week 4, SS 2,SS 4)
    a. Velociraptor
    b. Diplodocus
    c. Apatosaurus
    d. Ankylosarus

13. The _____ carried plates on its back and had a small brain
    (week 3,SS 3; week 4, SS 4; "Dinosaur Detective" song)
    a. Ankylosaurus
    b. Pterodactyl
    c. Stegosaurus
    d. Saltopus

14. A Mussasaurus "the mouse lizard," ate all of these things except _____.
(week 1, LA 1, SS 1; week 4, SS 4)
   a. fruit
   b. leaves
   c. dogs
   d. berries

Traditional Test Answer Key _____

   1. lizard
   2. extinct
   3. Triceratops
   4. Cretaceous
   5. False
   6. False
   7. True
   8. True
   9. True
   10. False
   11. b
   12. a
   13. c
   14. c

AUTHENTIC ASSESSMENT CENTERS _____

Center #1   *Materials:* pictures of Tyrannosaurus Rex, Diplodocus, Allosaurus, Triceratops, Zelociraptor, Apatosaurus, Syntarsus, and Ankylosaurus; 8 pictures of teeth (4 sharp fangs and 4 grinding molars)

Task: Using what you learned about the physical differences between meat-eaters and plant-eaters, decide which dinosaurs are plant-eaters and which are meat-eaters; match the dinosaurs up with the teeth they would use (sharp teeth = meat-eaters, dull grinders = plant eaters). (week 3, SS 7; week 4, SS 2, SS 4)

Center #2   *Materials:* tinfoil, crayons and paper

Task: Using what you learned about the characteristics of real dinosaurs, use the tinfoil to mold a real dinosaur. You may draw one with crayons if you do not want to use the tinfoil. Write two or three characteristics that make your dinosaur real. (week 3, SS 2; week 4, M 5)

Center #3   *Materials:* 3 signs with the words Triassic, Jurassic, Cretaceous; 3 pictures of dinosaurs (Saltopus, Lambeosaurus, and Apatosaurus)

Task: This is a six-person activity. Each person must have either a sign or a picture. The ones with the time periods must get in order and form a timeline from oldest to newest. The three students with pictures must match up to the period that the dinosaur on their card lived in. (week 3, SS 4; week 4, SS 2, SS 4)

Center #4   *Materials:* paper, pencils, crayons

Task: Pretend you have just received a letter that your dinosaur cousin Fran is coming to town tomorrow and wants to eat dinner at your house. Decide what type of dinosaur Fran is; then determine if she is a meat-eater or a plant-eater. Make a menu of at least three items that you will cook for dinner. She must be able to eat these items! (week 3, SS 5; week 4, SS 4)

Rubrics for Centers 2 and 4

Center #2

Expert—The student completed the task fully, matching ability level. The student understood the characteristics of real dinosaurs and demonstrated them fully and clearly in the model/drawing. The student wrote three or more clear descriptors of the characteristics of real dinosaurs. The product showed creativity and effort.

Standard—The student completed the requirements. The model demonstrated two characteristics in the model/drawing. The written descriptors were average and had one or two characteristics. The student put in enough effort to finish the task.

Novice—The student did not complete the task fully. The student demonstrated little understanding of the task. The model was incomplete and unorganized. The model demonstrated effort but no characteristics of real dinosaurs. The student only wrote one characteristic or unclear/irrelevant characteristics.

Center #4

Expert—The student completed the task fully, matching ability level. The product showed effort and creativity. The student demonstrated full understanding of the task by making the connection between plant-eaters/meat-eaters and the dinosaurs' diets. The student listed three or more food items that were appropriate for the dinosaur identified. The dinosaur was correctly placed into the plant-eater/meat-eater category.

Standard—The student completed the task but not fluently. The identified dinosaur was matched to the correct category of dinosaur; the selections of food items were appropriate but minimal. The task was rushed and lacked creativity.

Novice—The task was incomplete and unorganized. The menu was lacking more than two requirements. The menu may have matched the dinosaur diet category, but there was inconsistency throughout the task.

Checklist for Center #1

Matching Dinosaurs to Category of Plant-Eater/ Meat-Eater	Level of Performance		
	Strong	Competent	Weak
Understood concept of the categories			
Demonstrated skill with terminology			
Matched dinosaurs accurately			
Completed task with ease			
Became involved in task			
Developed classifying skills			
Used picture clues to aid classification			
Used previous knowledge to help solve task			

Checklist for Center #3*

Putting Time Periods in Proper Order and Matching the Dinosaurs to the Period They Lived In	Level of Performance		
	Strong	Competent	Weak
Understood the concept of a timeline			
Worked cooperatively to order the periods			
Used terminology in proper context			
Discussed periods with familiarity			
Correctly ordered periods			
Correctly matched dinosaurs to their periods			
Used previous knowledge to help solve the task			

*Teacher observation required.

VII. Resources Section

Children's Books

1. *A Dinosaur Ate My Homework.* Nelson, R. Jr., Kelly, D., Adams, B. Beyond Words Publishing Inc.
2. *Dinosaur Bob and His Adventures with the Family Lazardo.* Joyce, W. First Scholastic Printing.
3. *The Extinct Alphabet Book.* Pallotta, J. Charlesbridge Publishing.
4. *If the Dinosaurs Came Back.* Most, B. The Trumpet Book Club.
5. *Dinorella: A Prehistoric Fairy Tale.* Edwards, P. D., Cole, H. Hyperion Books for Children.
6. *Dazzle the Dinosaur.* Pfister, M. North-South Books.
7. *Dinosaurs at the Supermarket.* Camp, L. Penguin Books USA.
8. *Brother Billy Brontos Bygones Blues Band.* Birchman, D. F. Lothrop, Lee & Shepard Books.
9. *My Visit to the Dinosaurs.* Aliki. Crowell.
10. *Digging Up Dinosaurs.* Aliki. Crowell.
11. *Dinosaurs Are Different.* Aliki. Crowell.
12. *Dinosaur Bones.* Aliki. Crowell.
13. *Dinosaurs* (poems). Hopkins, L. B.
14. *Mitchell Is Moving.* Treasury of Literature.
15. *Do You Know How Dinosaurs Lived?* Benton, M. Warwick Press.
16. *What Happened to the Dinosaurs?* Branley, F. M. Crowell.
17. *Dinosaur Time.* Parish, P. Harper & Row.
18. *100 Dinosaurs From A to Z.* Wilson, R. Grosset.
19. *New Questions and Answers About Dinosaurs.* Simon, S. Morrow.

Videos and Films

1. *Dinosaurs.* Windows on Science, Volume 2.
2. *Dinosaurs.* National Geographic Society, 1978.
3. *Dinosaurs,* Parts 1 and 2, Educational Dimensions, Inc., 1975.
4. *The Search for Stegosaurus.* Educational Dimensions, Inc., 1975.

Speakers

1. Paleontologist (conditional)

Field Trips

1. Charleston Museum
2. Dorchester State Park

VIII. References

Fuller, M. *Dinosaurs and Prehistoric Life.* Grand Rapids, MI: Instructional Fair Inc., p. 44 (posters).

Dinosaurs, Macmillan Early Science Activities. (1991). Newbridge Communication, Inc., p. 44.

Karges-Bone, L. (1995). *Authentic Instruction and Assessment.* Good Apple, Morristown, NJ. pp. 86–87.

DAILY LESSON PLANS TAKEN FROM THE SRP

This section is for use with Chapter Five, in which directions are given for the design of daily plans. In this section, note the following:

- ✓ Measurable objectives
- ✓ Detailed procedures
- ✓ Accommodations for special learners and learning styles
- ✓ Assessment provided for each lesson
- ✓ Connection to the goals and objectives outlined in the SRP

NOTES ABOUT DAILY PLANS AND EXPERIENCED TEACHERS

The daily plans in this section contain a great deal of detail. They are for the purpose of instruction in teacher education courses or for modeling by novice teachers. Experienced teachers will probably not need or want to commit this much time to daily plans. However, these kinds of robust plans are essential for skill and practice by new teachers and for their administrators to review in evaluations.

EXPLORATION—ANTICIPATORY
CREATIVE ARTS LESSON PLAN #1 _____

Grade Level: Second

Subject: Introduction of unit

Objective: The students will be able to sing the "Dinosaur Detective" song.

Verification: South Carolina Visual and Performing Arts Frameworks—component 1: explore, identify, and move with variety (p. 56); component 2: differentiate between speaking/singing voice (p. 88).

Rationale: Many students learn through music. However, music is not incorporated into the curriculum as often as it should be. This lesson serves as the anticipatory set of the unit.

Materials:
- Magnifying glasses for each student
- Flashlight
- Tent
- Jungle music and CD player
- Assortment of tropical plants
- Words to "Dinosaur Detective" song
- Fossil shells
- Children's books (*Dinosaur Bones; Do You Know How Dinosaurs Lived?*)
- Scattered dinosaur clues or fossils around the room
- Automotive lamp inside tent

***A Very Good Management Plan!!!!!

Procedures:
1. The teacher will set up tent, dim lights, display plants, and turn on jungle music before students arrive.
2. The teacher will have a tan trench coat on and stop children before they go into the classroom.
3. The teacher will explain that for the next four weeks the class will become Dinosaur Detectives and learn all about these terrible lizards.
4. The teacher will describe the job of a detective as having to be quiet and observant so that no clues are overlooked.
5. The teacher will quietly lead students into the room and inside the tent.
6. The teacher will ask the students what types of clues Dinosaur Detectives might look for (fossils).
7. The teacher will explain fossils and show examples of fossil shells.
8. The teacher will explain that they are going to read a few books about fossils so the students can become expert Dinosaur Detectives.
9. The teacher will ask for student predictions and then read *Dinosaur Bones*. The teacher checks comprehension by asking questions: Are all bones the same? Do all bones become fossils?
10. After discussing the book, the teacher will introduce *Do You Know How Dinosaurs Lived?* and will explain that all the information about dinosaurs in this book was discovered by studying fossils.
11. The teacher will check comprehension by asking questions such as, was the earth the same then as it is now? How is it different? How is it the same?
12. The teacher will tell the students that they are almost Dinosaur Detectives but that they need to learn one more thing—the detective code.
13. The teacher will introduce the "Dinosaur Detective" song by displaying words and singing it through one time.

14. The teacher will then ask the class to join in.
15. The class will sing it a second and third time with the movements.
16. The teacher will then tell the students that they are official Dinosaur Detectives and must now receive a magnifying glass, which they must have with them at all times when they are at school.
17. The teacher will review the importance of fossils and then tell the students to look around the room for any prehistoric clues. (The integrated science lesson begins now!)
18. There will be no Early Finishers.

Assessment: The students will be assessed by observation, and their participation in singing will be noted in their anecdotal behavior records.

TRIASSIC PERIOD—INTRODUCTION
SOCIAL STUDIES LESSON PLAN #2 _____

Grade Level: Second

Subject: Plant-eaters versus meat-eaters

Objective: The students will be able to classify Triassic dinosaurs as plant- or meat-eaters, according to their physical characteristics.

Verification: Students are to be taught the process skills as specified by the *South Carolina Frameworks.*

Rationale: These students are highly interested in dinosaurs, and this activity is a good way to practice observation and classifying skills as well as to build unit vocabulary.

Materials: • Triassic Period poster
   • Pictures of Triassic dinosaurs
   • Banners/visuals (one describing meat-eaters, the other describing plant-eaters)
   • Mesozoic banner and Triassic banner to begin timeline wall

Procedures: 1. The teacher will have students review the role of detectives and discuss some recent classroom findings.
   2. The teacher will explain that, in order to be good detectives, they must know all the different dinosaurs and the time periods they lived in during the Mesozoic Age, or the "Age of the Dinosaurs."
   3. The teacher will describe the first period of the Mesozoic Age (Triassic) as warm, humid, and swamplike and will further describe the dinosaurs as smaller than later dinosaurs. The teacher will state that some were meat-eaters and some were plant-eaters.
   4. The teacher will introduce and describe several dinosaurs from the Triassic Period: Plateosaurus—largest dinosaur of this period; Syntarsaurus—possibly covered in feathers; Saltopus ("leaping foot lizard")—small dinosaur; Mussasaurus ("mouse lizard")—smallest skeleton ever to be found.
   5. The teacher will introduce the concept that not all dinosaurs could eat the same food. The teacher will explain that some ate meat and some ate plants, but none ate both meat and plants.
   6. The teacher will list characteristics of meat-eaters and put visuals on the board: sharp fangs, large claws, ability to have front legs upright when necessary, usually fairly fast.
   7. The teacher will describe the plant-eaters and put visuals on the board: long necks for reaching leaves; large, square teeth for grinding plants; usually some defense characteristics (large powerful tail, spikes, horns, plates).
   8. The teacher will ask if there are any questions.
   9. The teacher will divide the group into small groups and have them classify the Triassic dinosaurs as either plant- or meat-eating.
   10. The teacher will have students write the lists in their journals.
   11. The teacher will put up a picture of a Coelophysis and ask students to individually classify the dinosaur as plant- or meat-eating and write their predictions in their journals.
   12. The teacher will reveal that the Coelophysis is a meat-eating dinosaur and ask students to check their predictions.

13. The class will verbally review the characteristics of plant- and meat-eating dinosaurs and decide which dinosaur type they would like to be (introduction to math lesson begins.)
14. There will be no Early Finishers.
15. Remediation Students will practice the different characteristics of plant- and meat-eaters, using flash cards.

Assessment: The students will be evaluated according to their ability to:

Work cooperatively in groups.

List two or three correctly classified dinosaurs while working in groups.

Recognize the characteristics of meat- and plant-eaters in their individual dinosaur classification activity.

DINOSAUR PET
LANGUAGE ARTS/CREATIVE ARTS LESSON PLAN #3 _____

Grade Level: Second

Subject: Writing

Objective: The students will write a dinosaur pet story using vocabulary words, quotation marks, and dialogue words.

Verification: South Carolina English Language Arts Frameworks, standard #7 (p. 14), states that students will use language in a variety of forms; standard #10 p. 15) states that students will communicate effectively in various forms.

Rationale: Students love humorous and outrageous literature. They also like to write about themselves. This lesson combines both of these facts, which will increase the chance that students will enjoy this writing activity. Through this activity, their ability to demonstrate competence in English will improve, and the lesson reinforces communication skills.

Materials:
- Children's book: *A Dinosaur Ate My Homework*
- Vocabulary word list (extinct—no longer living on the earth; dinosaur—terrible lizard; prehistoric—before man; plant-eaters—eating only plants; meat-eaters—eating only meat)
- Construction paper, crayons

Procedures:
1. The teacher will review the story *Mitchell Is Moving* and review the skills of the lesson: antonyms—opposite-meaning words; dialogue words—said, yelled, whispered; quotation marks—punctuation marks used to enclose words and sentences that are spoken by a character.
2. The teacher will review vocabulary words (see materials) and ask students to volunteer to use them in a sentence.
3. The teacher will introduce the story *A Dinosaur Ate My Homework* by asking students to predict the plot and then say that it is a story about a boy who acquires a pet dinosaur after the dinosaur eats his homework.
4. The teacher will read the story and continually check for comprehension by asking questions: Do you believe a dinosaur really ate the boy's homework? Can you remember whether any of the dinosaurs mentioned in the book are ones we've already learned about in class? What would you do if a dinosaur ate your homework?
5. The teacher will ask students to think of a dinosaur they would like as a pet. What would it like to eat? What could it do to get you in trouble? Is it a nice dinosaur or a mean dinosaur?
6. Closure: The teacher will ask students to write in their journals about their pet dinosaur. The teacher will state that they must use dialogue words, vocabulary words, and quotation marks whenever possible in the story.
7. The teacher will monitor behavior and offer assistance.
8. The teacher will proof Early Finishers' work and have them draw illustrations for the scenes. (Creative arts lesson begins.)

Assessment: The students will be evaluated according to their ability to:

Write a clear story about a dinosaur.

Use all the vocabulary words.

Use dialogue words and quotation marks in appropriate places.

DINOSAUR MATH
TIME LESSON PLAN #4 _____

Grade Level: Second

Subject: Time

Objective: The students will be able to show times on a manipulative clock and write times in their workbooks, when given oral and written time facts during a review.

Verification: South Carolina Mathematics Frameworks states in standard #5 (p. 43) that students should be able to make and use measurements.

Rationale: Time is usually taught at the end of the semester/year, and it is often skipped in order to "catch up." Time is a concept that these students must be able to master at a very young age. By using manipulative clocks and integrated lessons, students will be able to make meaningful connections and learn this concept fully.

Materials: • Manipulative clocks
              • Children's book: Dinosaur Time
              • Workbook sheets

Procedures: 1. The teacher will guide a discussion about the book *Dinosaur Time* that the students read earlier.
              2. The class will discuss how they use time in their lives (going to school, eating, etc.).
              3. The teacher will review the function of the little hand (hours) and the big hand (minutes).
              4. If necessary, the teacher will review that there are twenty-four hours in a day and that the small hand must pass the number 12 twice to have a whole day (12 + 12 = 24).
              5. The teacher will explain that when a time fact is written on the board, the students are going to show that time on their clocks.
              6. The teacher will demonstrate to the class in order to clarify directions.
              7. The class will do this review and practice until most of the students understand the concept.
              8. The students will then do independent practice in their workbooks while the teacher works with Remediation Students.
              9. Early Finishers may read silently, add to their dinosaur stories, or work at math centers.

Assessment: The students will be evaluated according to their accuracy and completion of their practice worksheets. The students will be visually assessed by the teacher according to their ability to tell time on manipulative clocks.

DINOSAUR SCIENCE REVIEW
END-OF-UNIT LESSON PLAN

Grade Level: Second

Subject: Review dinosaur facts

Objective: Students will be able to recall and describe many dinosaurs and their characteristics.

Verification: The *South Carolina Science Frameworks* state that characteristics of living things and their interaction with the environment should be taught in this grade. Standard #1 (p. 41) states that science should be learned through active involvement.

Rationale: This game is in the format of a spelling bee. It is not going to be highly competitive, but it will get students involved in reviewing dinosaurs. This quick-paced activity will ensure that students will review almost everything they learned about dinosaurs.

Materials: • Dinosaur period posters
              • Completed time line
              • The Big D Challenge review sheet

Procedures: 1. The teacher will ask if the students enjoyed being Dinosaur Detectives.
              2. The teacher will ask students if they learned anything about dinosaurs.
              3. The teacher will explain that they need to review everything they have learned so that they can remember it for a long time.
              4. The teacher will tell students they are going to play a game similar to a spelling bee.
              5. The teacher will explain that whoever answers the question first will stand by the student to the left. If that same student also answers the next question first, that student will move to the next person. However, if the other student answers the question first, than that student will move to the next person. This will continue until all the questions have been answered correctly.
              6. The teacher will demonstrate the rules three or four times and then start the real game.
              7. The teacher will establish order and maintain class structure.
              8. There will be no Early Finishers.
              9. This is for Remediation Students as well as for fun.

Assessment: This is based on students' participation and teacher observation of who was unable to answer at least half of the questions.

Glossary of Planning Terms

Academic goals: Broad, overall outcomes for student learning in the areas of reading, writing, language arts, science, social studies, mathematics, geography, and the fine arts.

Accommodations: Specific procedures and strategies used to help children participate fully in instruction or to enable children to have access to activities.

Activities: Refer to tasks, games, songs, or any kind of "doing" in which the children learn. Activities are not procedures. Activities are included as part of a procedure statement.

Affective goals: Broad overall outcomes for student attitudes and behaviors in areas such as citizenship, manners, work ethic, appreciation for learning, and self-confidence.

Anecdotal record: A document on which the teacher records observations of specific student behavior. This may be used for documentation in a due process for special education or as a form of authentic assessment to share with parents.

Assessment: The evaluation of student learning and of the success of instruction.

Auditory discrimination: The skill of listening for and interpreting fine differences in sound (in early childhood, a prereading skill).

Auditory learner: A child who learns best by listening and asking questions.

Auditory memory: The ability to remember what one has heard (listening skills).

Authentic assessment: Form of assessment that allows children to demonstrate what they know and are able to do, usually through some sort of project, creative task, or hands-on method.

Bloom's taxonomy: Refers to the six levels of questioning defined by Dr. Benjamin Bloom (knowledge, comprehension, application, analysis, synthesis, and evaluation).

Centers: Specific, individualized learning activities or groupings of material that enable children to practice skills at their own pace and through the use of manipulatives, games, or toys.

Checklists: A simple form of assessment in which teachers and/or students use a list of behaviors or skills to keep track of individual or class performance.

Closure: The process of wrapping up a daily lesson, usually in the form of the last procedure described in the daily plan.

Cognition thinking: The process of acquiring new knowledge and using previous knowledge in unique ways.

Content (concepts): The knowledge delivered in the curriculum (facts, dates, names, reasons, or theories).

Convergent question: A test item or question used in a procedure on the daily plan that has only one correct answer.

Cooperative learning: A form of instruction in which pairs or small groups of children complete a task together, drawing on individual talents and abilities to enable the group to succeed.

Criteria: Specific behaviors or descriptors used to score student work.

Curriculum: A description and framework of the knowledge and skills that students are supposed to learn and apply, and any materials that support that pursuit.

Daily plan (lesson plan): A narrow, specific piece of the short-range plan that delivers one objective.

Deductive thinking (reasoning): A process in which the child moves from thinking generally about a concept to forming a more specific understanding of the concept.

Description of students: A process and product in which the teacher investigates and analyzes the student group in order to figure out the best way to plan for instruction.

Discipline plan: A concise, pragmatic description of how the teacher will manage classroom behavior and noninstructional activities so there is a safe, engaging learning environment with a maximum of instructional time.

Divergent question: A test item or question used in instruction that has a number of possible correct answers. It is also known as an open question or open-ended question.

Duration of instruction: An estimation of how long the teacher and students will work on specific objectives or sets of objectives. It may be found in daily plans, short-range plans, and long-range plans.

Early Finishers: Children who complete work early. A procedure in the daily plan may accommodate those children who complete the lesson ahead of others. The Early Finishers' procedure should review or enrich the stated objective. Homework or centers can be an acceptable directive for Early Finishers.

Elementary level: Refers to grades 2–5.

Enrichment: Procedures designed to meet the needs of children who show advanced academic ability or to encourage creative thinking skills among all students.

Expressive language: In the primary or early childhood curriculum, refers to a child's ability to use language verbally (*see also* Receptive language).

Fine-motor activities: In the primary or early childhood curriculum, refer to activities, including holding a crayon, pencil, scissors, or paintbrush, that enable children to develop control over small or fine muscles.

504 plan: A document outlining special accommodations for children who have a medical, mental, or physical impairment or problem that interferes with their ability to learn in the regular setting (Section 504 of the Rehabilitation Act of 1973).

Gender-based instruction: The process of matching instructional strategies to the differences demonstrated by boys and girls in the ways that they learn. These are biological-cognitive differences as well as social differences.

Gross-motor activities: In the primary or early childhood curriculum, refer to the development of large muscles through learning activities (skipping, jumping, throwing a ball, or left-right directions)

IEP (individualized education plan): A federal document mandated by PL 94-142 and the IDEA describing the objectives, goals, and assessment of student learning for children with disabilities. There are thirteen categories of special education funding.

Inductive thinking (reasoning): A thinking process in which a child moves from specific observations to a more broad generalization.

Inference skills: A form of higher-order thinking in which children use clues from what they have seen or read to form an opinion or to answer a comprehension question.

Inquiry: A method of instruction in which questions are used by both the teacher and student to acquire knowledge and understanding of concepts.

Instruction: All of the methods, procedures, teacher attitudes, teacher skills, and teacher behaviors used to deliver the curriculum to students.

Kinesthetic-tactile learner: A child who learns best by trying something.

Language arts: In the elementary curriculum, refers to listening, speaking, reading, writing, and grammar. In some areas, reading instruction is included. In other areas, reading instruction is planned for separately. The LRP and SRP should specify whether reading is covered in the language arts strands.

Learning style: Refers to a host of descriptors that are used to explain the unique ways that children learn. Some of these include visual, auditory, kinesthetic, left-brained, right-brained, global, analytical, deductive, inductive, active, passive, hands-on, and multiple intelligences.

Literature (children's literature): Refers to the use of picture books, children's books, juvenile novels, and magazines that support and enrich instruction. An optional list of children's literature is often included as an addendum to the SRP. In some states, teacher evaluation instruments require this addendum.

Long-range plan: Also known as the LRP. It is a narrative and schedule that maps out the instructional and affective territory that students will cover over the course of a semester or year.

Long-term memory: Information that has been stored in a part of the brain that keeps it safe for future use or the recall of information after days or months.

Manipulatives: Small items, such as counters, beans, puzzle pieces, crackers, buttons, or building toys, that can be used to help children learn concepts in mathematics. In science, manipulatives typically refer to the use of any material that children can put their hands on during a demonstration or experiment, such as magnets, beakers, or even a magnifying glass.

Materials: Any rescues, manipulatives, textbooks, speakers, centers, books, magazines, technology, or reference materials used in the delivery of instructional objectives.

Methods: Strategies and techniques employed by the teacher to deliver instruction. They may include hands-on, questioning, lecture, discovery, inquiry, experimentation, research, demonstration, cooperative learning, individualized instruction, supportive corrections, drill and practice, or exploration.

Multiple intelligences: Refer to Dr. Howard Gardner's model of how the brain of each child allows for separate, specific strengths in eight areas: linguistic, musical, visual-spatial, bodily-kinesthetic, interpersonal, naturalistic, logical-mathematical, and intrapersonal.

Objective: A specific, measurable learning outcome.

Parent communication: Refers to a plan for maintaining ongoing communication with parents as well as individual methods for such communication (newsletters, notes, phone calls, postcards, conferences, e-mail, and bulletins).

Phonics: A method of reading instruction based on the memorization and linking of sounds to form words.

Planning matrix: An open-ended document that enables the teacher to write down or brainstorm ideas for instruction.

Portfolios (portfolio assessment): A collection of student products or tasks that are used to demonstrate growth over time or to document weakness in an area of the curriculum.

Primary level: Refers to grades K–4.

Procedures: The part of the daily plan in which the teacher describes what will be done or set up to enable the delivery of instruction of the objectives to the students. Procedures should be specific and include activities as well as questions to be asked, information about duration of the procedure, and use of materials in the procedure.

Process skills: (science): Terms used in the assessment of science performance and in science instruction (observation, classification, data gathering, measurement, inference, and communication).

Questioning (see also, Deductive thinking, Inductive thinking, and Inquiry): A strategy used in instruction and assessment to find out what children know or to move the lesson along to a new point. Questions should be listed in the procedures of the daily plan.

Rationale statement: Found in the LRP, SRP, and daily plan. This statement is the teacher's personalization of the curriculum. It is a form of explanation and justification for why and how the interaction is delivered.

Receptive language: In the primary or early childhood curriculum, refers to a child's ability to hear and understand the spoken word (*see also* Expressive language).

Review: A strategy for going over previous concepts and skill learned before proceeding with new instruction. It may be found as the first and/or last procedure in the daily plan. Review may also be scheduled prior to assessment checkpoints in the LRP or SRP.

Rubric (also called a scoring rubric): Specific guideline for scoring a product, task, or performance. Frequently, points or numbers are given for a certain level of expertise.

Sample (model) plan: Refers to the LRPs and SRPs offered in this book that demonstrate the techniques for planning.

School-to-work plan: An optional component of the SRP in which the teacher describes lessons or activities that would help children connect the stated objectives to their relevance in the real world or to specific career choices. In some states, this is a requirement in teacher evaluation.

Scope and sequence: A chart or matrix that spells out the order of concepts to be delivered at each grade level.

Short-range plan: Also known as the SRP. It is a set of lessons and accompanying goals, assessment, and rationale that cover a period of instructional time of two weeks or longer.

Short-term memory: The recall and reproduction of material after a brief period of time (minutes or a few hours).

Social studies: In the elementary school curriculum, refers to six areas for which teachers are responsible: geography, history, economics, civics or government, anthropology-sociology, and political science.

Socialization: A term used in primary or early childhood education to describe strategies for helping young children learn to demonstrate courtesy, respect, use of materials, and self-direction during the school day.

Special needs students: Students whose physical, mental, emotional, or social abilities are such that they require accommodations in pacing, materials, or methods in order to be successful. This grouping may include learning disabled, physically challenged, attention deficit or hyperactive, gifted, talented, visually or hearing impaired, language delayed, medically fragile, or emotionally disturbed children.

Standards: Refers to national or state-level benchmarks for student achievement (e.g., *S.C. Frameworks for Science* or the *National Geography Standards*). Typically, national standards have been developed and approved by a subcommittee of a professional organization (the National Council of Teachers of Mathematics) or by a state department of education task force. Standards are used to verify the appropriateness of content.

Support for special needs students: Specific procedures built into the daily plan to help all students participate in instruction.

Technology plan: Refers to the use of computers, television, video, radio, CDs, laser discs, or other forms of technology used in the delivery of instruction.

Traditional assessment (test): A form of assessment in which students respond to specific, usually convergent, questions designed to measure their mastery of a defined set of concepts.

Unit: A collection of daily lessons connected by a common theme (SRP). It is also called an integrated unit.

Validity: An assessment term that describes the extent to which a test measures "what it is supposed to measure."

Verbal fluency: A child's ability to use language with ease at the appropriate level for chronological age.

Verification statement: Found in the LRP, SRP, and daily plan. This is the teacher's system of checks and balances. The teacher verifies the concepts and objectives against what the district guidelines or objectives, scope and sequence from the textbook, or national standards require for the grade level.

Visual discrimination: The ability to classify and discern letters and shapes in textual context.

Visual learner: Aa child who learns best by seeing or reading.

Visual memory: The ability to remember the shape, name, and placement of letters or shapes.

Vocabulary: Listed in the procedures section of the daily plan and as an option in the SRP, refers to specific words or terms that children should be able to use expressively and receptively in order to understand or master the objective.

Vocabulary development: Strategies or programs used to increase students' mastery and flexibility of language.

Writing process: Refers to the steps used to teach writing: brainstorming, first draft, proofreading, editing, and publishing. Some teachers simply use this term to refer to any aspect of a formalized writing program.

Bibliography

Ashton-Warner, S. (1963) *Teacher*. New York: Simon & Schuster.

Ayers, W. (1993) *To Teach: The Journey of a Teacher*. New York: Teacher's College Press.

Benjamin, H. (1939) *The Saber-Tooth Curriculum*. New York: McGraw Hill.

Chappell, F. (1989) *Brighten the Corner Where You Are*. New York: St. Martin's Press.

Collins, M. (1990) *Marva Collins's Way*. Los Angeles, CA: J. P. Tarcher.

Conroy, P. (1972) *The Water Is Wide*. New York: Bantam Doubleday Books.

Dewey, J. (1938) *Experience and Education*. New York: Macmillan.

Gardner, H. (1984) *Frames of Mind*. New York: Basic Books.

Holt, J. (1967) *How Children Learn*. New York: Dell Publishing Company.

Johnston, L. (1992) *My Posse Don't Do Homework*. New York: St. Martin's Press.

Karges-Bone, L. (1994) *Teacher's Reports of the Effects of Authentic Assessment on Instruction*. Columbia: University of South Carolina.

———. (1995) *Authentic Instruction and Assessment*. Morristown, NJ: Good Apple.

———. (1996) *Beyond Hands-On: Techniques for Using Color, Scent, Taste, Touch, and Music to Enhance Learning*. Carthage, IL: Teaching and Learning Co.

———. (1998) *Middle Grade Assessment*. Torrence, CA: Good Apple.

———. (1998) *More Than Pink and Blue? How Gender Shapes Your Curriculum*. Carthage, IL: Teaching and Learning Co.

Kleinbeau, N. H. (1990) *The Dead Poet's Society*. Madison, WI: Bantam Press.

Kliebard, H. (1992) *Forging the American Curriculum 1893–1958*. New York: Routledge Press.

Lortie, D. (1975) *Schoolteacher: A Sociological Study*. Chicago: University of Chicago Press.

Marshall, C. (1967) *Christy*. New York: Avon Books.

Montessori, M. (1966) *The Secret of Childhood*. New York: Ballantine Books.

National Commission on Teaching and America's Future. (1997) What Matters Most: Teaching for America's Future. Available from http://www.tc.columbia.edu/teachcomm.

South Carolina Department of Education (1996) *ADEPT Guidelines: South Carolina System for Assisting, Developing, and Evaluating Professional Teaching*. Columbia, SC: Department of Education.

Sylwester, R. (1995) *A Celebration of Neurons*. Alexandria, VA: The Association for Supervision and Curriculum Development.

INDEX